HUSBANDS:
An Endangered Species

RONALD N. HAYNES PUBLISHERS, INC. is committed to publishing significant works with new ideas and re-publishing time-tested works that can change the world in the name of Jesus Christ.

If you who have picked up this book are a Christian, you have experienced the joy and challenge that Jesus brings to life. If you are not a Christian, read on—you may see why so many people throughout the ages have entered the family of the forgiven and found there both peace and purpose through Jesus Christ.

HUSBANDS:
An Endangered Species

By

Lucille Lavender

Ronald N. Haynes Publishers, Inc.

PALM SPRINGS, CALIFORNIA

Husbands: An Endangered Species

Copyright © 1982 by Lucille Lavender

 Ronald N. Haynes Publishers, Inc.

PALM SPRINGS, CALIFORNIA 92263-2748

Library of Congress Catalog Card Number 82-081143
ISBN 0-88021-071-0

Printed in the United States of America

How poor, how rich, how abject, how august,
How complicate, how wonderful is man!
from *Man*, "Night Thoughts"
by Edward Young, 1683–1765

Table of Contents

Acknowledgements

I want to thank the reference staffs of the following libraries that were my "life support system":

University of California Library, Santa Cruz
University of California Library, San Diego
California State University, Northridge
California State University, Bakersfield
Kern Health Science Library, Kern Medical Center, Bakersfield
Los Angeles Public Library, Los Angeles
Santa Cruz County Library, Santa Cruz
Fuller Theological Seminary Library, Pasadena

The courtesy and helpfulness extended to me by librarians and assistants was outstanding.

A very special thanks to the Beale Library Reference Staff of Kern County Library, Bakersfield, who graciously and tirelessly helped me research countless pieces of information and answered hundreds of questions via telephone thereby saving me much time and inconvenience. They include:

Sandra Siercks, Gloria Washington, Mary Haas, Mary Hanel, Hapi Winheimer, Dee Mooneyham, Catherine McCullough, and Louann Nickerson

To my editors, Judy Headley and Carolyn Fritsch who unrelentingly, yet supportively, refused to let me strive for anything less than excellence, I am most grateful.

Lucille Lavender

HUSBANDS:
An Endangered Species

Chapter 1

Husbands:
In a Race for Survival

*Grant that I may not so much seek to be under-
stood as to understand . . .*
                              St. Francis of Assisi

For nearly three years I have been thinking, sleep-
ing, eating and finally writing about the plight of husbands whom I not facetiously call an endangered
species. "Ours is a disposable society," an acquain-
tance observed. "We dispose of food leftovers, cloth-
ing worn a few times, hamburger cartons, cars,
Pampers, churches (I'll find one I like), why not husbands?" She was kidding—I think—but as I pondered
her half-way humorous comment, it struck me that
like so many consumer commodities, husbands have
been tossed into a modern quick-frozen, defrosted,
micro-waved, instant, and pre-packaged "market"
where, incredibly, they are still called upon to meet
centuries old expectations based on the assumption
they were "predestined for dominance." Husbands
have been stereotyped into roles: hunter, warrior,

bridge-builder, law giver, ruler of the world and the home, and the appointed pursuer-aggressor in the bedroom.[1] They have been expected to keep their cool, not have moods, not to have close friends, and not to let it all hang out; to keep climbing Jack-and-the-Beanstalk's ladder, which never quits growing, to the top.

Husbands are expected to be in charge of themselves, their jobs, their wives, their kids and their feelings. At the same time, they are controlled by the clock, their superior, their employer, their union, their income, their health and their neighbor, who paints his house yearly and cleans his garage weekly! His wife can have her period or her change of life and therefore be "entitled" to crying spells, moods and locking herself in the bedroom, but he cannot. Why? Because she's woman. And he's man!

The multiplicity of complexities which face twentieth-century husbands were demonstrated to me when I phoned my friend, Dr. Donald Forden. His little daughter answered brightly, "Hello!"

"Hello," I responded. "Is Dr. Forden there?"

Pause, "No, but my daddy is. Daaaaa-dee!" she called loudly. I heard the extension phone picked up.

"This is Daddy—uh—Dr. Forden!"

As he shared later, in that delightful, humorous exchange a finely tuned human computer had ticked away in his head. Who am I? A person? A father? A man? A daddy? A doctor? A friend? A citizen? A mind? A body? A spirit? A soul? A chain reaction of emotions? The fact is, he is expected to be all of these, and more, as prescribed by society. As Dr. Forden answered my "hello" he had to quickly switch roles. In the eyes of society, it is far more significant to be "doctor." But in the eyes of his little girl, it was far more important to be "Daddy."

These outside forces, pulling this way and that, impose themselves so violently upon husbands that their life expectancy is eight years less than that of their wives. For generations husbands have been on a treadmill exchanging hats and roles—daddy–doctor, husband-fixer, leader-helper, carpenter-lover—with little, if any, "inside permission" to be just plain human. As if that were not enough, less than a generation ago a bomb exploded. War was declared. Women went on the march. The sexual revolution picked up where it had stopped a century ago. But this time there would be no armistice until territorial rights had been clearly established. Many of the reasons for this revolution were sound and justified. And many men I know agree with women who say, "for conquer we must; the cause, it is just."

But there is more to it than that. Intellectualizing about equal pay for equal work and women's strength and mental acumen to perform many of the tasks men do, may be an entertaining weekend diversion. However, living it out is another matter. On Monday morning, when husband goes to the office to find his new "boss" a woman; when he begins his shift at the fire station and sees a woman in "his" uniform nurse a baby; when he leaps up the high step of the semi to reach the driver's seat of "his" cab, and is told to go around to the other seat, because today Mary will drive the route—he is shocked to discover that "his" world is no more! His territory has been invaded. The privacy of his domain—the driver's seat, the locker room or the name plate on the office door—has been invaded. He feels caught. He has no escape cover. His environment has been changed. Who needs a hairbrush over a sun visor, or a cosmetic drawer in an executive's desk, or a female tossing up hundred-pound sacks at the loading dock? He is totally disoriented. His male-ness is threatened. His masculinity is questioned.

Husband then goes home to his haven, his private castle. Some place in this crazy world, his ecosystem must find some balance. Surely, at home, he will find things the way they were. Wrong! Wife wants to go to work. She is tired of being a cook, maid, baby-sitter. She wants challenge, excitement, and mental stimulation in her life. And, in our present economy, fifty-one percent of all wives must work. So husband doesn't find "sense" or balance at home either. When wife comes home from work, she is as tired as husband, though she may not earn as much as he does. She asks, then demands that husband help, because "I work just as hard as you do all day long." And the battle is on.

Wife desires and deserves a hand with the children, the dinner, the laundry and the dishes. Though many men go along with the idea of a working wife, often husbands cannot handle menial "woman's work." That should not be difficult for wives or husbands to understand. Certain ideas have been impressed upon all of us from childhood as to husband's role. Every son models himself and his marriage after what he saw his father (and mother) do, whether he likes it or not. Every wife models herself after what she saw her mother (and father) do, whether she likes it or not. We are all victimized by the "grown-ups" (who may be fairly mature, or extremely immature) who raised us, whether we like it or not. We all come into this world like empty blotters which soak up the input of those "in charge" of us.

The husband who draws no distinction between "man's work" and "woman's work," and who genuinely enjoys helping around the house, often finds it difficult to handle the added input which comes when his wife attempts to share the day-to-day happenings on her job. She wants and needs his interest in matters that concern her. However, he may already have all he can cope with mentally, physically and emotionally. Hearing her problems and the machinations of her job scene, added to his own pressures, flips his psychic overload switch. His emotional transformer strains to carry the added burdens, but his ability, even willingness, to express love and involvement is seriously diminished. Sometimes it shuts off completely and there is a temporary communications blackout.

The purpose of this book is to help bring awareness and insight to wives about some of the problems facing their husbands in the technological and sexual revolution of the last decade and of the eighties. The changes have been profound, earthshaking and soul deep, reaching to the core of how we all think, feel and decide. Women have been saved from the frustration of living down to expectations and role-stereotypes which kept them from becoming all they were meant to be. But husbands deserve saving, too. Women can use their new found freedom to help accomplish this worthy goal. For if husbands, too, are not set free, they will indeed be endangered. In fact, I believe they are an endangered species. And, thereby hangs the survival of the human species!

Zealous environmentalists man boats to stalk the shores of Canada and the United States in order to "save the whales." Young men and women throw human walls around pup seals to prevent their slaughter. Environmentalists spend hundreds of thousands of dollars to appeal to our merciful instincts to save the beautifully ugly rhinoceros and manatee from destruction and extinction. I heartily support these efforts, for we now know that if strong measures are not taken, we will lose much of the earth's spectacular wildlife.

Many nations, rich and poor and with varying ideologies, are working together to stop the steady disappearance of plants, fish, birds and mammals. They are cooperating to stamp out a flourishing international traffic in rare animals and products manufactured from them. There has been a sharp cutback in the hunting of whales, the largest living creatures remaining. Many countries are creating preserves and animals parks. Stringent laws have been set up for those who traffic in rare animals, and stiff penalties are imposed on violators. It is beginning to pay off. There have been stunning successes as an impressive number of nearly extinct species have been restored and preserved. And for others this process is beginning.

But where is the hue and cry for the endangered human species? Where are the boats, full of the young, the old, the people who are concerned about saving the species known as *husband?* Until recent years it has been taken for granted that there is a male for every female born; that is to say, a husband for every woman who desires one. But that concept has been drastically altered by today's realities. Species *husband* is in a race for survival!

One can go to almost any kind of mixed gathering, whether in a concert hall, theater, church, restaurant, retirement center or convalescent home and become aware that the ratio of women to men is considerably larger. Through observation, research, interviews and casual conversations, I have learned that the majority of these women, whether single, divorced or widowed, indicate in some manner that they would like to have the full commitment of one man, and particularly, commitment within the context of marriage. But the species *husband* eludes many of them.

Not every woman has this deep desire or need, and many who do may never have a husband. This does not detract from their personhood, nor does it diminish their value to God and society. Many single women have distinguished themselves admirably. They have a special freedom to pursue vocations because, perhaps, they do not have the consuming responsibility and demands of marriage.

In 1966 the Congress of the United States passed the Endangered Species Preservation Act which ruled that:

A species of native fish and wildlife shall be regarded as threatened with extinction whenever the Secretary of the Interior finds . . . that its existence is endangered because its habitat is threatened with destruction, drastic modification, or severe curtailment, or because of other factors, and that its survival requires assistance.[2]

Drastic modification of wildlife habitat has dramatically curtailed wildlife population. Modification includes the cutting of forests, the cultivation of untamed wilderness for expanding cities with their residential and commercial developments, and the continued building of roads and super-highways. This leaves less and less habitat and escape cover in which animals feed, rest, play and breed. Without a habitat conducive to these activities, there can be no assurance of future generations of the species.

Disease caused by a polluted environment is on the upswing. Predation by the higher orders over the lower orders has always been nature's way to keep wildlife population in balance. But the newest predator—man—has become the most fearsome enemy, with his indiscriminate slaughter and poaching for personal gain or pleasure. Some species of the large kingly animals, such as the elephant, asiatic buffalo and Indian tiger, are now numerically in the low thousands. Other magnificent animals are in the hundreds or less. The snow leopard and Indian cheetah are extinct.[3]

As described earlier, husbands are endangered for reasons not unlike those which threaten wildlife. Husbands, too, have suffered over-exploitation, drastic change to their enviroment, pushing back of their "habitat," pollution, disease, and weakening of the species by stress.

A professional man in his forties, who considers his marriage of twenty-three years a good one, made a remarkable commentary on the present-day scene. "I have sensed for some time that a hidden rage is building within men in our culture, because men feel desperately trapped, and don't know how to act. Women may not realize it, but they exert enormous emotional control over men. Men want to please women. But all the rules are being changed."

The purpose of the Endangered Species Act is to provide a program for the "conservation, protection, restoration, and propagation of selected species." If nations around the world with differing, even opposing, ideologies can band together to conserve, protect, restore and propagate endangered wildlife, wives can learn to think and live in a manner designed to insure the survival of the species *husband*. Now, more than at any time in history, while "all the rules are being changed," women can use the freedoms they have won to set their men free from expectations and stereotypes which have held *husband* hostage far too long. It is important to save endangered wildlife. However, it is of far greater importance—though difficult at times, and, at times, intensely rewarding—to "conserve, protect, restore and propagate" this very special endangered species called: *husband!*

Chapter 2

Husbands:
The Stronger Sex?

His life was gentle; and the elements
So mix'd in him . . .

Julius Caesar
William Shakespeare

Some years ago, when my brother took his little boy to the dentist for the first time, the youngster was terrified. Both father and dentist did all they could to reassure him. But son of brother was not convinced by these attempts to make him something other than he felt he was.

"I'm not a brave little man," he protested through quivering lips. "I'm a scared little kid!"

How much of the scared little kid is hidden inside many of the big brave men in our society? And why not? Although candor would admit that the freedom to ask this question is of recent vintage, we are learning, none too soon, that men, like women, have "weak" as well as "strong" components in their nature.

11

Historically, man occupied what appeared to be a "favored-status" position. Compared with the typical woman of even a few years ago, he had more options, more power and more freedom in his choices. We are discovering that for this supposed "favored-status" position he has paid a terrible price. Though equipped with a larger frame, and larger heart and lung capacity, he also suffers more heart disease, ulcers, alcoholism, and goes to an earlier grave than his female counterpart.[1] The exciting world "out there" proves to be a jungle from which few men return intact.

One husband comes to mind. He was an educator and, though his vocation was demanding, he enjoyed his work and had good health. He and his wife had an unusually harmonious marriage. A happy, fulfilling retirement lay just over the horizon. One morning, after they had breakfasted together and discussed plans for the evening, he kissed her goodbye and left for work. Less than two hours later she received the devastating news that he had been found slumped over his desk—dead.

Weeks later his wife talked with me about him, about them. "It was all going so well for us. Our plans, our savings, our health. We thought we had the attrition factor licked, because I was several years older than he." My friend's statement was based on the fact that today the female life expectancy is nearly eight years higher than that of the male, and increasing.[2]

Right now there are sixty-seven men for every one hundred women over the age of sixty-five. If this trend continues, by the year 2000 there will be one hundred forty women for every one hundred men over the age of sixty-five.[3] Under these conditions the elderly would have to take up polygamy if women wish to have husbands.

There are exceptions, of course. Some women have never desired marriage. Some are in religious orders and professions. Others whose marriages have failed are disillusioned. They are finding fulfillment in other ways, especially in careers. But the fact remains: the majority of women—single, divorced, widowed, young, middle-aged, older—would like to have husbands. This was endorsed again recently at a VIP reception of a large corporation to which my husband and I were invited. An attractive, intelligent woman in her early forties, formerly married, and a vice-president of that corporation, was delightfully candid about her life and her desires.

"I would really like to be married," she confessed. "But I want to be able to say to a man whom I might marry, 'I don't need you to pay my bills, make me a complete person, give me babies, or a sense of self-realization. But what I would really like to have would be someone to share with—my joys, my failures, my successes, my sillinesses and my feelings. I don't need someone to lean on. I would like someone to walk with.'" She stared off into space. "But that's impossible to find."

In 1920 the death rate for both men and women was approximately the same.[4] Since then women have gained nearly a decade of life expectancy over men. As with wildlife, there are natural causes which bring about death, catastrophic illnesses and diseases related to growing older. But there are unnatural causes which may bring about some of the catastrophic diseases. They are the "hidden killers" and they are not diagnosable like a toothache, or appendicitis.

"That males are showing these dire longevity statistics must be viewed from the perspective of lifestyles, stresses, physiological habits, emotional responses, and sociological pressures."[5] More unsettling is the emerging realization that the endangerment of a husband does not begin on his wedding day. It begins the day he is born or, perhaps more accurately, in the womb.

What is happening to the species? What is the species doing to itself? What are women doing or not doing that endangers the species?

In most countries of the world, male babies are the most desired. The United States, though not as extreme, also shows this preference. In interviews with 1500 married women and nearly one-fourth of their husbands, almost twice as many preferred boys to girls. Responses to the interview questions revealed a behavioral pattern in this and other studies. Couples are more likely to have more children if they have only girls. They will have more children than planned in order to try to have a boy. Reasons given were to carry on the family name and to be a companion to the father. Those women who preferred girls wanted to put them in pretty dresses and fuss over them.[6]

"Sex is the first fact announced at birth and a salient concern throughout pregnancy," comments Lois W. Hoffman in *American Psychologist*. "In fact, sex differences in socialization, or at least the foundation for those differences, might be seen as existing prior to the child's birth. . . . The parents may not be aware that the sex of the child is affecting their behavior toward the child . . . the infant labeled female seems fragile, sweet and pink to the new mother, and she may not know that she is responding differently to her daughter than she would if the child had been labeled male . . . or when the father watches the toddler careening precariously on the top of the jungle gym . . . the male child's physical prowess and daring may . . . keep (the father) from expressing the anxiety he feels for the child's safety."[7]

It is as early as this in the life of a male baby that his anxiety and stress-producing conditioning begins. When a boy baby arrives on the scene, the "need-for-a-boy" syndrome may place upon him at the moment of his birth an expectation overload which he may never be able to meet. Newborn boys are more roughly handled than baby girls, because cultural sex-stereotyping dictates they are sturdier. But, in fact, female babies are more mature and more resistant to disease. In addition to rougher handling of boys, parents encourage boy toddlers to move around and explore farther away than girls. Boys are encouraged to be more independent and to take greater risks at an earlier age than are girls.[8] Male babies are viewed often as angry when they cry, while girls are considered fearful.[9] Boys are given more technically complicated toys than girls are, and these are also stereotyped according to "boy" and "girl" toys. Girls get playthings like dolls and miniature household equipment, while boys get mechanical trucks and building materials.

In preschool years, sex roles are one of the most pervasive concepts children will learn. Observers in a study noted the responses to prespecified stimuli in nursery schools and day-care centers. Boys were more aggressive, and girls more dependent. This aggression factor enters into a child's development in infancy. The structure of children's play and work roles encourages boys to be aggressive and girls to be ladylike. Boys invoke fewer negative responses and many times receive encouragement for imitating or initiating aggressive behaviors,[10] while girls are taught to be helpless and dependent.[11]

Finally, it is time to send the male-stereotyped, rough-and-tumble, aggressive, independent and, supposedly, in control of himself and his environment, product called "boy" off to the big, wide world—school. How does our boy fare in his new environment? LaVerne R. Graf, Program Specialist Consultant for Special Education in the Sacramento Public Schools in California, has researched this question. She was a classroom teacher for eighteen years, five of which were in an EH (Educationally Handicapped) class. For three years she served as resource teacher for fifty-five classrooms and assisted in preparing individual programs for 600 educationally handicapped students. She now monitors twenty-six classrooms and three hundred student programs, including learning disabled, autistic, orthopedically handicapped and developmentally-delayed children. She found that of all children in her district's learning handicapped classes, and throughout the U.S., between eighty and ninety percent are boys. The reasons for this are still being debated, but she agreed with the findings of others above concerning the learned role behavior from birth to kindergarten.

In addition to role stereotyping, there are several probable causes for boys' problems in school. They mature later but are subjected to the same pressures to achieve academically that girls are. Teachers of early grades are usually women who pay more attention to and positively reinforce the well-behaved, quiet girls, than the restless, squirming boys (who were taught to be aggressive). Graf also found that values in early grades reflect the feminine role in society—cautious, not daring; ladylike and orderly. Boys find more satisfaction and gain more attention by being disruptive, and therefore are given more attention than when they are "good." In the home, mothers are inclined to say, "Oh, he's just a boy!", while father has a "macho" image of what a "real" boy should be: a high achiever scholastically and a super-athlete in sports. When displeasure or punishment is shown, a boy is supposed to take it "like a man." The conclusion of LaVerne R. Graf, who has conferred with hundreds of teachers and parents, was that rarely does a parent talk about a son's sensitivity, his tenderness or sentimental nature. Rarely is a boy hugged, touched, caressed or kissed. That is considered "feminine."

The pressure of this classroom dichotomy affects boys far more adversely than girls. Three times more boys than girls are sent to child guidance clinics.[11] Autism and other mental illnesses are three to four times greater in boys. Schizophrenia is diagnosed forty-two percent more frequently in boys under age fifteen. Up to age twenty-four the male suicide rate is three times higher than that of the female.[12]

These are some of the discoveries about males which are the reason for the question mark after the title of this chapter—Husbands: The Stronger Sex? At one time they may have been stronger, or at least have been perceived as such. But these facts say that at this time, they are probably not. It seems as if society goes all out to create an extra amount of debilitating pressures on our men. What little boy has not heard:

What are little girls made of?
Sugar and spice and everything nice.
What are little boys made of?
Snips and snails and puppy dog tails.

Think of the impact on that small psyche from these "clever" little sayings. Girls are made up of nice things which make them cute, loving, neat and nice. All positives! Boys are made up of bad things and that is why they are sloppy, ugly, dirty, obnoxious and not worthy of being loved. All negatives!

A friend of mine, a family counselor, and I had a discussion about the socialization of boys. Speaking as a psychologist, he expressed concern over how boys are unconsciously taught to fit into role expectations far beyond them, and are then put down if they fall short. He verbalized feelings which plague men for life: "Girls have it made. Mommy loves them. Boys are supposed to take care of them and not fight with them even if harrassed. When it's time for dating, the boy has to make all the arrangements, and the girl takes and takes because she has been trained to do so.

"Girls are pampered and coddled even into adulthood. I confess to a nagging resentment every time I go into a men's restroom. It is without fail smelly and messy, even in some of the most expensive restaurants. There are no shelves, and dirty mirrors. Women's restrooms are usually cheery, bright, light, decorated and have places to sit or even lie down. I cannot recall any men's restroom with those amenities. I personally feel insulted every time I go into a men's restroom facility."

The combined effects of boy stereotyping and handling, aggressive behavior conditioning and putdowns which follow men into adulthood, and the constant continuing repression required for "masculinity," are some of the "hidden killers" of our men, our husbands.

Man has been given to this planet, and to woman especially, to fulfill a real and deep need in her and in himself. To construct a system whereby one man and one woman are to be committed to each other for a lifetime is a compliment from the Creator to the crown of His creation—man and woman. A compliment of the highest order!

To help sustain that lifetime commitment for the longest period of life is the commitment of this author and this book. It is time for women everywhere to make a stand against these "hidden killers." Surely a good place to begin is for each woman's prayer to be: "God grant me the serenity to accept the things I cannot change, courage to change the things I can, and wisdom to know the difference."[13]

Chapter 3

Husbands: Their Territory Threatened

Know then thyself, presume not God to scan,
The proper study of mankind is man . . .
Created half to rise, and half to fall;
Great lord of all things, yet a prey to all . . .
Alexander Pope

Husbands no longer are definable as they were a generation ago. "Once it was possible to define them by their advantages: physically, superior to women, psychically more stalwart, men seemed to be predestined for dominance. They were the hunters and warriors, the bridge builders and lawgivers, the natural autocrats of the breakfast table and oligarchs of the bedroom. They worked and earned for their families, came home to hot meals and compliant wives, took their ease in the privileged fellowship of the locker room and the all-male club."[1]

This is no longer the case. Male, single or married, is in a battle for survival. The world which he used to

know once had a semblance of structure and predicta-
bility. But that world—his former domain—is in a
state of chaos. Almost nothing which was dependable
yesterday can be counted on today. That alone would
be enough to shake the strongest man's confidence!

Just as humans have been constantly encroaching
on the territory of wildlife, husbands are now finding
their territory threatened. In more primitive times,
geography, the elements, other tribes and peoples
limited a man's domain. In the civilized world, on his
job, in the factory, in the ranks of management, his
territory has been reduced by economics, social structure, abilities and education.

In very recent times another force complicates husband's attempts to maintain his territory. Changing
roles present seemingly devastating threats to the
previously sacrosanct role of traditional husbanding.
Woman no longer wants to be under man's domination. She insists she does not need his protection. The
female he singled out, courted, married and impreg-
nated to produce after his kind, is doing an about-
face. She has had a taste of independence and she
likes it. She has proved herself capable in many areas
heretofore considered "for men only." Technology
freed her from the kitchen, and the "pill", from the
nursery. These changes are invading more and more
territory traditionally revered as belonging to the
male. An important part of this change is the feminist
movement, or women's liberation. Whether this
movement is considered good or bad, right or wrong,
desirable or undesirable is not at issue here. The over-
riding reality is that it has brought about radical, pro-

found change, and continues to bring about more.

It did not suddenly happen out of the blue when some "radical females" called men emotion-laden names and demanded "rights." What people do not understand, they fear. Therefore a short history of the feminist movement should help men and women, wives and husbands, to understand when and why the movement first began. Perhaps some prejudices will be eliminated on both sides of the issue, and help bring about more reasonable attitudes.

Throughout history, societies and civilizations have established and abided by cultural mores which characterized them. Some ancient societies were matriarchal, or matrilineal, and some of these survive in the present. In matrilineal societies, women and their progeny are the ones who dominate and govern.[2] But most cultures were patriarchal, that is, dominated by the male. Under most systems of ancient law, a woman in a patrilineal society, no matter how old, was theoretically a minor. She was always subject to control by her father, her husband or other male guardian.[3]

The agrarian nature of most civilizations dictated woman's "proper place." Not only did she tend the household and bear the children which were necessary to the survival of society, she also worked in the fields to help bring in the food supply. This is still true in parts of the Middle East and Asia. Women of the ruling class fared better, though useful only to enhance and give pleasure to their men. Those of royal blood were treated like pawns, and were traded like cattle to foreign royalties for political favors and peace treaties.[4]

The first organized women's rights movement in the United States began in 1848 as a direct outgrowth of the slavery struggle. While working for the freedom of slaves, women became aware of their own lack of freedom to speak publicly, work outside the home, to receive an education or to vote. Today's women's liberation movement reflects the struggles of that period.

In pre-Civil War days, "woman's proper place" was in the home. She bore and nurtured the children and attended to her household as women had done for centuries. This was known as the era of the *maternal wife*. It reflected values of motherly affection and love. One of woman's primary concerns was to instill obedience in her children. In some ways it was a relatively enlightened era in which she was guide and friend as well as mother.

In the late nineteenth century there were some changes in the perception of woman's sexuality. Largely through the efforts of Margaret Sanger, a flaming personality who flaunted all existing mores, the contraceptive issue charged into public consciousness. Attention focused on sex and the bedroom. To counteract this, "bedroom laws" were hastily enacted in the 1870's which prohibited the use of contraceptives and abortions. Sexual procedures were spelled out in the legislatures of many states—some still on the books. Woman found herself with the responsibility of keeping these laws and of maintaining sexual virtue. As Sheila Rothman points out, this became the era of *virtuous womanhood*.[5] Women led purity crusades condemning the use of contraceptives. Social purity legislation taught that the male was a savage beast who would corrupt woman to satisfy his animal impulses. One female writer insisted that marriage was the capturing of a wild animal, whose taming was to be the life work of the wife.[6]

Some women reformers, physicians and clergy taught that abstinence was the only permissible way to limit childbearing, and that sexual expression was harmful, but might be permitted occasionally. Since woman's mission was basically motherhood, sexual over-indulgence only debilitated, distracted and corrupted her. The goal of the *virtuous woman* of the late nineteen hundreds was primarily to purify and tame her husband and society.[7] Medical authorities further defined her role and abilities, as well as disabilities, during this period. The female psyche was emotional, and therefore precluded activities in the outside world. Menstruation was considered debilitating and even harmful. Some medical advice from that time stated, "Long walks are to be avoided . . . also long wheel rides—in fact, all severe physical exertion. Intense mental excitement as a fit of anger or grief or even intense joy may be injurious."[8]

"That women were at once the more civilized, the more moral, and the more virtuous of the two sexes, and at the same time the victims of precarious health (and temporary insanity), made for an odd duality of traits."[9] Despite this, the mind of woman was being stimulated, and a network of women's clubs, reform associations, and philanthropic societies such as the WCTU and YWCA were founded during this era.

With the coming of the twentieth century a new definition of proper womanhood emerged—*educated motherhood*. For the first time women took training on how to raise their children, which had previously been considered "maternal instinct." This led to the rise of child and maternal health clinics, kindergartens, new types of schools and improved working conditions for women. They focused on achieving higher education, and the right to enter businesses and the professions. Women's suffrage was achieved after fifty years of struggle, persecution and ridicule, when, in 1920, Congress passed the Nineteenth Amendment granting women the right to vote.

In the 1920's, the concept of woman moved away from primarily mother to *wife-companion*. It was a romantic and sexual definition, moving women from the nursery to the bedroom, though wives were still expected to remain at home. In these movements from one era to another, the concept of woman from the previous period was not automatically dropped. I believe that the best of each of these definitions of woman are still with us today: *maternal wife, virtuous woman, educated motherhood* and *wife-companion*.[10]

The First World War and the Great Depression put the women's movement on hold for several decades, but dynamics were at work which paved the way for the modern feminist: the virtual demise of the small family farm which sent people to the cities by the thousands and World War II. Suddenly a clarion call was sounded by none other than the United States government. Men were needed to fight the war. Would the women go to the factories and make the weapons?

Woman was catapulted suddenly into man's world. And though she would continue to be the mainstay of her home, husband and children, she would never again be content to be confined to being just that! Woman discovered she wanted more than to view the world vicariously through her husband and children. She wanted to be out in it. She wanted to use her mind and abilities and stretch them. As a result, in addition to the *maternal wife, virtuous woman, educated motherhood* and *wife-companion*, one more type emerged. It brought the most radical changes of all in the struggle for women's rights. It was *woman-as-person*. It was the woman who wanted her own identity!

The spark that ignited the most recent and radical phase of the women's revolution started with the publication of a book. Sensing frustration, emptiness and a basic loss of identity for women, author Betty Friedan zeroed in on these problems. Blame had previously been attributed to lack of sexual fulfillment, advanced education and a surrender of femininity. Friedan, however, saw it differently. She perceived the problem as society embracing the all-pervasive "Feminine Mystique," the title of her book.

This mystique dictated that woman's only commitment was to fulfill her femininity, and that she was to be solely wife and mother. "Women tried to be like men, instead of accepting their own nature, which can find fulfillment only in sexual passivity, male domination, and nurturing maternal love," or so the theory went. The mystique meant that women would find fulfillment because of their biological inferiority, by living vicariously through their husbands and their children. Anything that thwarted this mystique—her housewifely adjustment—caused all her problems.

Friedan objected to this view and placed the blame on women's lack of identity. "It is my thesis that as the Victorian culture did not permit women to accept or gratify their basic sexual needs our culture does not permit women to accept or gratify their needs to grow and fulfill their potentialities as human beings, a need which is not solely defined by their sexual role."[11] The book struck a chord. It sold two million copies, and the modern women's liberation movement was off and running.

There are six major forces which have converged since World War II to set the scene for the rebirth of women's liberation in the sixties, and provided fertile ground for its success:

Life expectancy In 1900 the average woman had a lifespan of 46 years.[12] After she raised her children, if they survived disease or accident, she would die. To-day, the average woman has a life expectancy of 76 years. She now has 30 years of life after her children are raised.

Technology Automatic washers, dryers, microwave ovens, home computers and other incredible gadgets still on the drawing board, have given woman the gifts of queens—luxury and leisure time.

Mobility The family has reached a state of near-frenzied mobility and division. Over forty percent of the population moved in the latter part of the seventies.[13] The extended family, consisting of divorced parents, grandparents, uncles and aunts and other units, is scattered across the country, leaving a feeling of emptiness.

Adult Education The information explosion made it imperative for adults to continue to learn, both for finishing or continuing education, and for learning new skills useful in the job market.

Affluence The automobile (two or three for every family), the airplane and television enlarged woman's horizons, and she wanted to experience the world opened up to her through the affluent society which allowed her to have access.

Inflation The high cost of living has driven woman into the job market. For half of the wives in our country, working is not an option, it is a necessity. And they want better jobs and better pay like their male counterparts.

The women's movement did not create these factors, and change would have come for everyone, without an organized movement. The feminist movement merely speeded up a process which was inevitable. It also demanded the kinds of rights and privileges and opportunities which might not have come otherwise—for women, particularly. But the effect on husbands has been devastating. The endangered species has been pushed into a corner with his back to the wall. This is especially true of traditional sole-source-of-income husbands. It is tough competing successfully in the job market with other men. For many husbands it is doubly difficult when their role as bread winner is threatened by a woman seeking to

expand her horizons and expecting—in some instances, demanding—"affirmative action." If she
works to provide only a second source of income to
her family, while he functions as sole provider, his
being passed over in favor of a promotion for her can
be infuriating, especially if she is not demonstrably
more competent than he.

A twenty–seven–year–old union member was selected by his employer—a large, multi-national corporation—for a junior executive slot. The competition
had been tough, but he prevailed over several appli-
cants, including one woman. The personnel manager
was honest, however, in telling him, "If the economy
worsens you will be a prime candidate for dismissal."
When he asked, "Why?" he was told, "Because you
are young, white and male."

He explained later, "I have always supported the
women's movement and I still do. I must admit I
would find it easier to be 'let go' in favor of an older
employee with company seniority, but I believe I
could handle dismissal in favor of a minority person
or a female, unless I knew I was more qualified. Then
race or gender shouldn't be considered. If they were
the deciding factors, I'd find that hard to cope with."
He paused, looked thoughtfully at me and said, "I've
decided to take the job even though I lose a degree of
security in leaving my union, and I'll give a 110 percent to make sure I'm a better employee than any I
may have to compete with." As I listened I said a
quiet "hurray" while inwardly wondering what
added stress, if any, this fighting on four fronts (other
men, older employees, minority persons and women)

would generate for this young idealist.

Katie, a sharp thirty-year-old executive, expressed genuine concern for the "good old boy" truckers she evaluated for productivity in her former role as efficiency expert for a nationwide trucking company. "It really blew them away when I climbed into the cab and began doing a time and motion study of them. Some would shrug and say with a sigh, 'I knew it would come to this someday. But why me?' Some would tell me to go to 'you know where' until I pulled rank on them and then they'd acquiesce in a quiet rage you could almost feel. Some treated me condescendingly as if I were their daughter or girl friend until I started making suggestions for more efficiency. And then 'the banana hit the fan!' Some assumed I was 'on the make' to even want such a job and my wedding ring plus comments about 'my neat husband' left them bewildered. A few—very few I might add—were highly supportive and treated me like the professional person I am. For most of the truckers, however, my riding along was unnerving. I understood where they were coming from, but I had a job to do and I was determined to do it as well as I could despite their macho hangups!" A not so quiet "hurray" for her, too. If any woman can minimize the threat, this lovely five-foot-four bright-eyed brunette can. However, it would be naive to say that her presence in the traditional male "preserve" of eighteen-wheelers is not threatening.

The feeling of insecurity is not limited to blue collar workers, as Katie discovered when she was promoted. "My present job puts me in contact with VP's in this and other companies. I'm finding more of a 'dumb broad in the wrong industry' attitude among executives with comparable education to mine than I did among men on the dock with limited schooling. Most of their wives have never worked. They resist my receiving equal pay for equal work when mine is a second source of income and they are sole providers. I tell them, 'Send your wife to work if it bothers you that my husband and I earn as much as we do.' I had expected resistance to a woman on the docks but I've been surprised by the attitude of my fellow managers. Many of them are really uncomfortable at seeing a lipstick, brush and mirror in an executive's desk!"

Some white collar workers are demoralized when the "man's world" of upper management is invaded by competent women. "I had been pointing toward vice-president for thirty years and then, just when it was in my grasp, they 'leap frogged' this lady over me," a disgruntled, fifty-eight–year–old retired bank manager told me. "She may have been as talented as I," he admitted grudgingly, "but she didn't have near the experience." His face clouded as he asked, "How do you think I felt when I had to go home and tell my wife and kids my lifelong ambition would go unrealized because 'affirmative action' called for a woman V.P. in our bank?" Without waiting for a reply he volunteered, "I was humiliated."

He quit—"took early retirement" it's called—shortly thereafter, only to learn within a matter of months that the woman was not ready for the responsibility she had been given, and had been transferred to a smaller branch where she could gain the necessary seasoning. Some might find it easy to fault him for wrong thinking or rotten attitudes. It's not up to me to either approve or disapprove of the way he handled his experience with the "feminist invasion." Knowing his age group, conditioning and expectations I can, however, get inside his feelings. Feelings have no morality, we are told. It's what we do with them that counts. And I agree. But surely the most ardent feminist can understand how traumatizing it was for him to have devoted thirty years of efficiency and loyalty to his employer only to have his "last plum" plucked out of his grasp by something so impersonal as a government directive.

Husband's territory *is* threatened. Implied in the word "threat" is an indication of impending danger; a person or thing regarded as a possible danger. Its root word means to "squeeze." Husband feels all of these feelings—pushed, scared, devastated, demoralized—endangered as he is by someone "new": woman. He feels squeezed, compressed, and fearful. And fear leads to anger. He feels he has been pushed too far, too fast. He may want to accept this new order, but not with reluctance, nor on demand, or out of feelings of shame and guilt. He must be given space, and time, to absorb and understand what has happened, and to accept, with some sense of peace and good feelings about himself, the fact that change has been realized by women because much change has been needed.

He is going through his own "quiet revolution." "Nobody is marching," states Betty Friedan in her latest book *The Second Stage*, in which she, herself, has swung to a newly found "moderate" stance. "American men are at the edge of a momentous change in their very identity as men . . . It is a deceptively quiet movement, a shifting in direction, a saying 'no' to old patterns, a searching for new values, a struggling with basic questions that each man seems to be dealing with alone . . . He feels awkward, isolated, confused. Yet he senses that something is happening with men, something large and historic, and he wants to be part of it."[14]

Husband and wife must learn that shared responsibility; for protecting, providing and participating in family life should have a positive effect, by reducing stress and by creating a happier, healthier, more balanced ecosystem for both male and female of the species. If a wife helps her husband to understand what is happening, and if she helps him to keep his sense of personhood and masculinity, he will be less threatened by the process.

After every revolution, society will be altered. Whether the resultant change is good or bad will be for the future to assess. In the current major confrontation between woman and man, wife and husband, the outcome will depend on how maturely they react to it, and to each other. And, in the interim, wives must learn how to use their new privileges wisely, if they care about saving their endangered species—their husbands. For husband, given space and time, may discover new dimensions to his own freedom and self-hood in the emergence of hers.

Chapter 4

Husbands:
Chauvinist or
Chauvinized?

The Child is father of the Man.

William Wordsworth

A little girl wrote a letter to God,

Dear God,
Are boys better than girls? I know you're a boy.
But please try to be fair.

Teresa

For centuries little girls, big girls and adult women have consciously or unconsciously, verbally or non-verbally, asked the question, "Are boys better than girls?" Centuries before any women's movement, surely generation upon generation of women must have reached the conclusion that men are not "better," that is, more favored, more endowed, more capable or "chosen." And, as today, women through the centuries responded in varying ways to the intuitive "no" they felt. They responded dutifully, accept-ingly, rebelliously, manipulatively, constructively, destructively and brilliantly, as an ancient biographer wrote about his extremely gifted and highly capable wife:

> A wife of noble character who can find?
>   She is worth far more than rubies.
> Her husband has full confidence in her
>   and lacks nothing of value.
> She brings him good, not harm,
>   All the days of her life.
> . . . and he praises her:
> "Many women do noble things,
>   But you surpass them all."[2]

In the preceding chapter a short history of the modern feminist movement was presented, and some of the causes which led to its inception. Many attitudes about women were confining and restrictive, though promulgated by social leaders, psychologists and physicians. Now we know they were more "notional" than scientific.

Many men feel good about the gains women have made and will continue to make. They take pride in the talents and capabilities which are coming to life in their wives and in other women. One of the major problems husbands have with the feminist movement is some of the abrasive methods which have been used to bring about change. In the early days of the movement (in the nineteenth century), women marched, carried signs, chanted slogans and showed their anger. However, the mores of the day dictated some sense of etiquette, some basic courtesy and dignity, even as they attacked men and male-dominated institutions.

Today's movement is considerably different. The 1960's were years of open rebellion and anti-every-thing, including the other person's right to personal dignity. Four-letter words and "let-it-all-hang-out" speech descended upon university campuses. It was in this atmosphere that the latest chapter of women's liberation began. The "radical" modern feminists, too, carried signs, chanted slogans, and, in addition, en-gaged in shocking language and shocking behavior which attacked the personhood—the dignity—of man, of husband. Included in the verbal attacks was a word which stuck—*chauvinist!*—from the degrading phrase, *Male Chauvinist Pig!*

Husbands—are they chauvinist or chauvinized? *Chauvinism* is defined in the dictionary as "excessive or blind patriotism, or undue partiality or attachment to an ideology or a cause."[2] To what "cause" or "ideology" are men so attached that they keep women in bondage? Some answer, "They have put women into stereotyped roles." When carefully scrutinized, however, the argument falls under its own weight.

It *is* true that since the dawn of mankind, women have traditionally been the center of the home. They have stayed near the hearth. They have conceived and birthed. They have nursed their young from their own bodies. They have fed, cleaned and nurtured their offspring. They have maintained the household. It is also true that since the dawn of mankind men have traditionally gone outside of the home to pro-vide food and sustenance for those inside. They have gone into the fields from sun-up to sun-down to till and cultivate and harvest. They have gone on the hunt for days and weeks to bring back food. They have tamed the animals, the horses and oxen, to help in their tasks, and the cow and the goat to give nourishment. The truth is, that both men and women were placed into stereotyped roles for reasons of sheer survival in what was, for thousands of years, an agrarian, not an industrialized, world.

In matrilineal societies, except for childbearing, the roles are reversed. Women's family names are perpetuated. The female sex is the distinguishing criterion. The descent lines which issue from the woman become the hierarchy, which governs and makes the clan or tribal decisions. Men raise the children and care for the home. Thus, both women and men are placed into stereotyped roles in societies where women rule. There is no evidence to indicate that these societies are less prone to problems than are patrilineal societies, or whether the women or the men are happier with their prescribed "roles."

As we become more enlightened, however, we are all coming to realize that no one should be oppressed by another. A woman should not oppress a man, nor man a woman. A master should not oppress another human being to be slave. A society should not oppress a race or a religion. One nation should not oppress another nation.

The problem of "chauvinism" is a live and forceful issue which needs cool clarification apart from emotional name-calling. Are all males and all husbands chauvinists? According to the definition which feminists have attributed to the word—*chauvinism* equals repression of women and a *chauvinist* is a male who deliberately tries to keep women from achieving equal status with men—some men probably are. From the creation of mankind to extremely recent times on the anthropological "clock," men and women had certain functions to perform out of sheer necessity to survive —literally. But the Industrial Revolution and now the Technological Revolution brought about incomprehensible and unbelievable change in methods of survival. The methods of these revolutions brought about major societal forces which would allow changes in role and life style for both sexes.

Up until now, a primary truth has been overlooked or ignored in the heat of battle: If men are *chauvinists*, they have been *chauvinized* to be *chauvinists*—by women! For the first ten years of his life a boy lives and learns primarily in a woman's world and in a female-ordered environment. He is taught by mother, baby sitters (usually female), day-care attendants, and teachers. He is taught, primarily by women, to grow up to be "masculine," independent, self-reliant, protective of his sisters and other girls, to play with "boy" toys, and be in control of himself and his environment.[4] His "environment" includes boys with whom he should be "aggressive," and girls whom he should "manfully protect."[5] He discerns very early in life, situations in which aggression is not only allowed, but is viewed as a sign of "manliness."[6]

Thus, husband, in the formative years, is thoroughly conditioned (chauvinized), primarily by women, to dominate his environment and those in it. He is chauvinized by the way he is depicted on the American scene. He is portrayed as the bungling television husband; the racy, violent hero of the cheap novel; the father whose advice can always be improved upon; the enemy of women who blame their problems on him; the cigar-smoking, greedy executive; the tough, cussing guy who pinches waitresses.

Husband is viewed by wife as basically uncomplicated—cool, calm, collected, fixer, accommodator—with few of the emotions she has. At the same time he is accused of being egotistical, shallow, insensitive and exploitative. He is the butt of denigrating jokes:

> He took her hand in marriage,
> But made the basic blunder
> Of letting her withhold from him
> A thumb to keep him under.

Though often wife pictures herself as submissive, compliant and passive, she brags about her manipulative practices, "I let him think he runs things, but I can wrap him around my little finger."

Husband is called an animal by his mother-in-law, a skunk by colleagues, a rat by competitors, a pig by feminists, and a stubborn mule by his wife. For centuries husband has been taught by society, which unwittingly taught woman and wife to teach him, certain "desirable traits."

To be an admired husband he must be:

> handsome of countenance and bearing
> powerful over those around him
> ruler of his kingdom
> provider of his household

indomitable achiever
courageous warrior
defender of his territory
protector of his wife, family and others
    of the female gender
aggressive paramour of the bedroom
decision-maker for his family
comforter of his spouse
master of his fate

Husband's role, strongly stereotyped and whether or not acceptable by moderns, was in the past clearly defined and virtually unquestioned. But today the "desirable traits" list has been increased and revised, and sends out dual messages.

To be an admired husband he must be:

good-looking, but not aware of it
strong, but not tenacious
protective, but not fawning
intelligent, but not heady
mechanical, but not grimy
masculine, but not overmastering
firm, but not inflexible
understanding, but not condescending
self-assured, but not conceited
loyal, but not patronizing
acquiescent, but not weak
passionate, but not demanding
humble, but not self-deprecating
ambitious, but not a workaholic
aggressive, but not pushy
neat, but not fastidious

gentle, but not feminine
knowledgeable, but not a show off
communicative, but not garrulous
agreeable, but not a yes-man
even-tempered, but not boring
helpful, but not under foot
defending, but not suffocating
generous, but not extravagant
relaxed, but not lazy
courageous, but not foolish
loving, but not maudlin
sexy, but not too often

To which of these simultaneous messages should husband respond? Each of the "musts" is watered down by a "must-not!" One husband expressed his near despair, "I know who I am. I have a good self-image. I love my wife very much. But for years in my marriage I have been struggling with double messages. What does my wife want me to do and be as we relate to each other? I wish I knew."

It is just plain tough for a man, for a husband, when he comprehends (or fails to comprehend) that woman births him, raises him, desires him, seduces him, entraps him, and then attacks him as Male Chauvinist! Not surprisingly, men are not only despairing and confused, they are angry. They react strongly too, as they probe the meaning of "me, man, male, husband and my rights!" Many lash back by rejecting the whole idea of husbanding and committing themselves to one woman in marriage. They are scared of making themselves vulnerable to "darling wiles" which might become "damning wails."

Natalie Gittelson, an author and supporter of the feminist movement, interviewed hundreds of men, Gentile and Jew, rich and poor, working-class and middle-class, about their feelings and reactions to the advancement of women. She wrote a book about her findings. Below is a quote from it:

> There were angry and anxious men: men who, dreading women, masked their dread in exaggerated displays of deference or, according to one psychologist, hid behind the smoke screens of "studied neutrality"; highly motivated and highly charged . . .
>
> With astounding frequency, American men used the vocabulary of exhaustion, inadequacy and defeat to describe the way they felt about themselves. Many said, "insufficient," some said "superfluous," others "unnecessary," or "superseded," "overwhelmed," "overshadowed," or "out of control."[7]

Dan, a middle-management bachelor in his early forties, whom I met in a social gathering, became highly talkative when I questioned him about his feelings toward women as it related to the feminists description of male chauvinism. "Men have been neutered. Grown-up women still consider themselves to be 'sugar and spice.' They are taught to be secretive, manipulative, alluring, and to communicate without a word. Men—grown-up little boys—are eternally 'snips and snails.' A boy gets his feelings about women from women, mostly from mother. She shapes all of his eventual relationships with women. And, at each stage of life, he must again deal with women."

To Dan "all-out war by 'female chauvinists' is unacceptable," although he seemed to understand the need for women to be given the same opportunities as men have. "However," he went on, "when women make war on males they are as bad or worse than men. 'Female chauvinists' seem to enjoy intimidating, threatening, and emasculating men. They fight unfairly. They accuse men of asking sexual favors to climb up the business ladder, yet they wear low-cut dresses, shiny lipstick, and tons of mascara. Women say in essence, 'I am equal to you,' but then they use the 'inequality' of feminine wiles."

Dan said much more, but he finished with some food for thought: "Men have not deviously, cunningly devised the scheme of things. They have been stereotyped for thousands of years to be chauvinists, if that is what they are. Sometimes I think women want all the benefits of equality without the pain and struggle of responsibility. Strawberries and cream also have some grit! I am old-fashioned enough to honor and believe in the Golden Rule: 'Do for others what you would like them to do for you.' What's wrong with that?"

Years before the modern women's liberation movement I was "liberated" by an understanding husband who not only allowed, but insisted that I develop my own personal interests and talents. I have great empathy for women who have been denigrated, and who have not been allowed to pursue their own interests. But I have also been granted keen, perceptive and empathetic insights into some of the ways the women's movement affects the male, perhaps because of the understanding awarded me by my husband.

Stuffed into male sex role socialization—"You must be stronger, independent, masculine and daring," then shoved out into the big wide world with, "Remember, you are a man" (which translated means, be sure to hide your feelings)—husband has virtually no opportunity to be an infant-person, a child-person, a young man-person, an adult-person, or a husband-person because he had so little male infant, child, youth, adult, or husband modeling.

I keep coming back to the larger plan of everything, including the first husband and wife relationship: "And the Lord God formed man from the dust of the ground and breathed into his nostrils the breath of life, and man became a living being . . . The Lord God said, 'It is not good for the man to be alone. I will make a helper suitable for him. . . . For this reason (so man would not be alone) a man will leave his father and mother and be united to his wife, and they will become one flesh."[8]

It makes such very good sense. In their masculinity and feminity they could and would contribute to each other's personhood in the home and in the market-place. With Dan I must conclude, "I am old-fashioned enough to believe in the Golden Rule: 'Do for others what you would like them to do for you.' "

Chapter 5

Husbands:
It's O. K. to Cry!

Tell me what makes a man laugh and I will tell
you about his charms.
Tell me what makes a man cry and I will tell you
about his character.

Lucille Lavender

Sitting in a physician's waiting room one afternoon,
I put aside my reading after futile attempts to make
sense out of a paragraph for the eighth time. It was
useless. I looked up and found myself surrounded by
many small creatures. Obviously I had stumbled unknowingly into a land of little people not unlike those
who ensnared the legendary Gulliver. Somewhere
close, I ascertained, was a "big people" who went by
the name Dr. Pediatrician who would sooner or later
attend to the feigned or real needs of these "little
people."

Suddenly, a number of these beings discovered me.
By devious means, they gradually began to weave a
net around me. At first they shyly came close and

studied me. Then they began to point me out to fellow Liliputians. Others gathered around, and they joined in pointing, laughing, poking, pulling on my belt, and shooting spit-balls in my face.

My legs were crossed, and one little urchin put full weight on my foot which had been nervously rocking back and forth. A grubby little hand pushed a sticky lollipop into my gaping mouth. As I attempted to expel such, a scarf was pulled over my eyes. "Holy Toledo," I mentally protested, "They did it! They've got me!" My capture was complete. I slumped into submission. All that was left was the mop-up.

By this time a few harried, semi-comatose mothers came to the rescue, although reluctantly. It was obvious these poor souls needed any respite they could get, and I was fair game. As I studied the mothers' haggard faces and staring eyes, I gathered some compassion. It was the least I could do to alleviate their mother-trauma for a few merciful minutes. Gradually things quieted down as, to everyone's relief, one by one the Liliputians were called by name into nether regions beyond mysterious doors. I confess little concern about their fate, as I tried to pull myself back together.

Some time later I recalled some of the dynamics—behavioral patterns and conditioning—in the doctor's waiting room. There were new infants, toddlers, preschoolers and grammar school children. They were male and female, large and small, black, brown and white. I observed firsthand that in our culture it is all right for a girl to display "masculine" traits, but not for a boy to give in to "feminine" ones immediately after infancy stage.

A mother nursed her boy baby. He was dressed in tiny blue jeans and a football t-shirt. In between vigorous sucking and squallings she gently rocked him and urged him to nurse. When he was through nursing, she put him over her shoulder and patted him gently for the inevitable burp.

A little girl toddler fell down repeatedly. Each time she was helped up and smilingly encouraged to try again. A very young baby boy fell and hit his head on the corner of his mother's chair and put up a terrible howl. Mother got off her chair, pulled him close to her, kissed his hurt and off he went, secure in motherly love.

One little girl named Alicia was about four years old. She had been one of my tormentors and was tyrannical indeed. She was the run-to-mother-and-scream-hysterically type. If she could not have the satisfaction of poking my eye into my head, or one of the other Lilliputians did not give her her way, she ran to mother and screamed hysterically. Mother patted her head with "There, there, sweetheart, never mind—those boys are naughty. You are mother's little darling."

This "there, there" mother also owned a little boy. He could not have been any older than three years. Little boy merely looked uncomprehendingly at my misadventure into Gulliver-land. During the melee, however, one of the bigger kids grabbed something from him and knocked him down. The little fellow managed to get to his mother through an avalanche of tears and bullies, sobbing brokenheartedly. The mother gave him a good whack on the bottom, and shouted, "Stop crying! Boys don't cry!"

Another little boy, between four and five years old picked up an abandoned "I cry-I wet" doll, and carefully studied it. He turned it over gently and pushed the "I cry" and "I wet" buttons. Triumphantly he found out how the doll worked, and his face broke into a marvelous smile. He headed toward his mother to disclose his victory. She stood up to her tall five-foot-ten height, shifted her more than ample weight, and yelled at him, "Put that doll down, SISSY! Dolls are not for boys!" The "self" of that little child disintegrated before my eyes. As of that moment, the whole area of "feminine" feelings had been closed off, locked up tight, forever. Never again would the boy-grown-into-man consciously admit or practice feminine qualities. The process of withholding "inside permission" *from* himself—*to* himself—had begun.

Though there is some evidence of change, this is how our society trains our males to be "masculine" from cradle on. Boys learn the "masculine" ideal very early. In homes and day-care centers, one observes that after the age of four or five months boys are picked up and hugged less than girls. Thus at a much earlier age than girls, boys are discouraged from asking for human attention and are pressured toward independence and autonomy.

Marc Feigen Fasteau in *Psychology Today* significantly observes that, "By five or six, boys know they aren't suppose to cry, ever be afraid or, and this is the essence of stereotype, be anything like girls. That is why calling another boy 'a girl' is the worst thing one boy can say to another, and why little boys hate little girls. The strain of trying to pretend that we have no 'feminine' feelings of doubt, disappointment, need for love and tenderness creates fear of these emotions in ourselves and hostility toward women, who symbolize these qualities."[1]

Girls have more options than boys, while still retaining their femininity. They can play marbles or twirl a yo-yo, usually designated for boys. But a boy who jumps rope will be in for a teasing. Girls can wear dresses or pants, but imagine what persecution a boy would be in for if he wore a dress. Girls carry books in front, clutching them with arms bent to their chest. Boys carry books at their sides. Leg-crossing is definitely a mark of "masculine" or "feminine." Women cross them knee-over-knee, but no man had better do so. He must cross his legs over the ankle, or calf over the knee in a figure-four position. One man related how, at the age of twenty-seven someone told him he was standing like a woman when with hands on hips, his thumbs pointed *forward* rather than toward his *back*.[2] Mercy, what an offense!

All of these signals from a child's earliest recollections mark him for life. When boys are ridiculed, chastened and corrected often enough about doing things "like a girl," it is no wonder many of them grow up doubting their "masculinity," and, ultimately, their sexuality. Children learn behavior by imitation. When a boy has only females around him, and a father who is gone most of the time, or he lives in a single female-parent home, it is cruel to expect him to display traits that are commonly thought of as masculine. Stated simply, he has no male model to imitate.

Parents need to examine how they may be contributing to possible bisexuality or homosexuality in their children, whether male or female. For years we have taken "polar opposites," that is, rigid masculinity and femininity, as evidence of good emotional and psychological health. "High femininity in females consistently correlates with high anxiety, low self-esteem, and low self-acceptance. And although high masculinity in males has been related to better psychological adjustment during adolescence, it is often accompanied during adulthood by high anxiety, high neuroticism and low self-acceptance."[3]

A tender true story illustrates the toughness men are supposed to exemplify, and reflects the maxim that "boys don't cry."

Death Stuns Police Force

A handful of Bakersfield police officers going off the night shift sat around the coffee room saying little.

When they talked, the expressions were of disbelief and shock over the sudden death of Police Sgt. Patrick D. Vegas.

Senior patrolman J. D. Foreman was called out to assist an unusually heavy workload that night. "I went from my home to the accident and saw that motorcycle laying on the ground. It was really a shock to me."

Like Vegas, Foreman rides a motorcycle.

Another officer held back the tears as long as he could, then broke down. "I'm sorry," he said. "A cop isn't supposed to cry."[4]

Feeling is as natural to people, both men and

women, as is breathing. Feeling is experiencing life through the senses. It is true sensuality and involves sight, smell, touch, taste and hearing. Feeling through the emotions reflects itself in the form of joy, sorrow, reverence, hate or love. God put these experience mechanisms into our bodies so we could enjoy, through many dimensions, the wonders of his creation. But our culture has a way of demeaning feelings in everyone beginning in early childhood. And the word has gotten out that men particularly are not to use this extraordinary gift, this ability to sense, emote and feel. "Accepting the challenge (i.e., repressing his feelings) amounts to deliberate repression of basic sensory signals, sometimes almost to the point of emotional freeze-drying. Men learn to do it very well. Repression begins with the earliest consciousness of a male child, and it ends with the death of a man. In this way the Male Mystique develops, and it becomes integral to the male . . . The condensed version of the . . . male mystique is simply this: 'You're a man. Don't be really scared, but if you have to be . . . don't let anybody know it!' "[5]

At the same time that they are learning (because it isn't natural!) to repress the emotional, boys in our society are taught to express the physical. They should definitely be "athletic." They must throw a ball like a boy, not like a girl. As they grow up they should go into activities which are group-orientated, with a target in mind: to win the game; harass the coeds; join the army; fight the battle; and join the fraternity.

There is hardly a father who, when informed that

his wife is expecting, does not dream that his son will someday become a star football player. After the child is born, he may develop great shoulders, huge legs, strong arms and a powerhouse build, but he may also have the gentleness of a kitten. He may feel anguish if he accidentally steps on an earthworm. Yet, as he grows to maturity, it is considered "masculine" to ram his two-hundred-plus pounds with brute force into another human being. The tyranny of masculinity is real indeed for young males in western society.

Junior may resist out of fear of being hurt, or because he is gentle. Perhaps he inherited the unathletic genes of one of his parents. "Little David" may also face the disappointment and rejection of his folks because he does not enjoy smashing himself into a two-hundred-pound "Goliath." By trial and error, mama's "big boy" and daddy's "tiger" grows up like Topsy. He is supposed to be a "man," and to him that means he must not cry, he must not fear, he must not touch, nor be touched. His most influential models are his parents. And most parents have given up showing affection for each other by the time Junior enters puberty or reaches adolescence. Rarely, if ever, do they hug him or tell him as they tell his sister, "I love you, honey." Girls are more often, though not always, raised to touch, caress, feel, hug. Junior, however, must not be "feminized."

"There is a deep-seated hunger within us that no amount of food can satisfy," says Dr. Sidney B. Simon. "It is a hunger for the touch, the feel, the concrete reality of human contact. Quite literally, it is 'skin hunger.' . . . It's not hard to tell the difference between types of homes. Young people whose skin-hunger needs are satisfied tend to be open, warm and relaxed. Those who have been rarely touched at home often seem to be more withdrawn, prone to living in a fantasy world, even hostile. I am convinced they have a diminished sense of their own worth."[6]

Junior is lonely, rejected and does not have the slightest notion of who or what he is. In this state he topples into adolescence. "Courses" in dating are taught him in the neighborhood park and school locker room. From braggadocio, beer-drinking buddies, whose verbal elocutions usually surpass their actual verdant exploits, he learns about himself. Unfortunately, it is a poor "education". A librarian confirmed some the problems teenagers face when learning how to relate to the opposite sex. She told how one young man sheepishly returned a book which was improperly "borrowed." The cover read *How to Hug*. It turned out to be the missing Number VII Volume of an encyclopedia!

Most young males by non-learning in the areas of affection, feeling, caring, and touching go directly to, and beyond, the "hug" without discovering "how" to. They have been shushed out of crying. Their hands have been slapped from caressing (themselves or girls), without any attempt to help them understand their tactile needs. They have been given the body-is-naughty lecture. How can they possibly develop step by step into wholesome, affectionate relationships with girls, young women and eventually a wife?

A young man who lived in our home for a while

gave new insights into what the "masculine" ideal
syndrome is doing to the youth in our nation, a nation
which encourages young men to deny their "feminine" qualities. He was in his early thirties. Though
he had a mother, he virtually grew up in the streets
where no one dared be "sissy" or do things "like a
girl."

He went to war in Vietnam, partly out of restlessness, and partly to prove how manly he was. When
he came back, he joined one of the chapters of a well-
known international motorcycle gang. The members
prefer to be called members of the "club." No one
dared show cowardice or weakness of any kind within the club, with other club chapters, or with
"straight" people. Initiation into the club was drastic
and horrible by anyone's standards, including the
initiates. Any insult from anyone in or out of the club
was acted upon immediately and violently.

This young man did not attend his mother's funeral
because an important club meeting was called at the
exact date and hour of her memorial service. He could
not overtly mourn for her in any way. And he never
did until several years later when he managed to escape from the club.

Though the gang or club is an example of extreme
distortion of the values taught our young male population, here is a list of "commandments" of the Male
Mystique of the late twentieth century as perceived by
a male sociologist:

He shall not cry.
He shall not display weakness.

He shall not need affection or gentleness or
  warmth.
He shall comfort but not desire comforting.
He shall be needed but not need.
He shall touch but not be touched.
He shall be steel not flesh.
He shall be inviolate in his manhood.
He shall stand alone.[7]

My young friend and his club members, from what
he described, exemplified these "commandments" to
the letter. Some months after leaving the club, he was
saved in the most profound sense of the word when
he met True Man in the person of Jesus. He found a
new dimension—his spiritual self—and bit by bit this
saving resulted in finding other dimensions. He began to feel all of his feelings, to discover and express
all of his qualities—loving, caring, gentleness, other-
centered—and in the process he is becoming a balanced, whole man! He mourns for his mother now
and, at times, he cries. Because he knows it's O. K. to
cry.

The most powerful man who ever lived cried openly. One such occasion is recorded in what may be the
most famous verse in the Bible, comprising just two
words: "Jesus wept."[8] It is the shortest verse in the
Bible, which is probably why it is so well known. One
husband bared his heart, "It's not the fact that the
verse is composed of two words which makes it significant to me. It's what those two words convey.
How I wish I could cry like Jesus did. How I wish I
did not care who in the whole world knew about it!"

What a pity. This man has much. Yet he does not have the freedom to cry.

Look what feeling does for you. If you feel extreme cold, it is a warning you may get frostbite. If you feel extreme heat, it is a warning you may be burned. If you feel internal pain, it is a warning something may be physically wrong and needs attention. In courtship and early marriage, feeling plays an important part, and emotions are considered acceptable, in fact, necessary. Unfortunately, for too many men, emotions take flight a few months after the wedding to return on rare occasions. Feelings to most men become a negative, which translated means: be reasonable; be rational; don't get emotional; don't let your feelings show. This is sad, for such suppression slowly and steadily cripples a powerful God-given part of his personhood.

Wildlife species, when confined in zoos and animal parks, rarely stalk prey, show anger or express the sounds endemic to their nature. In captivity all their food is provided, and animals which prey upon them are put elsewhere. They are, in a sense, "killed with kindness," and they become listless and passive. They do not behave like their species in the wilds.

In the "captivity" of a male child's upbringing, which suppresses and represses the normal show of emotions, it is not surprising that after the "hunt," "capture" and "mating" with the female, male as husband retreats into his past conditioning. This is one of the major frustrations the wife expresses "after the honeymoon is over." It is also the reason for this chapter. A wife needs to realize her husband may not converse with her after a day's work; he may not show affection "except for sex;" he may seem withdrawn and make her feel "alone." The wife must realize how difficult it is for her husband to become talkative, affectionate, emotional and teary-eyed at a movie or during grief, when he has been trained to "keep his cool; be a man!"

A wife can help her husband immeasureably in this area if she keeps her cool; if she does not go into a corner and pout. She can nuzzle his neck, put her arms around him, ask questions nondefensively about his day at work, and literally ask him to cry when he hurts. And he hurts often and deeply! Probably wives have been too mindful of how they feel, and too unmindful of how their husbands feel! Because feelings are not expressed does not mean husbands do not love them!

In other parts of the world men readily express their feelings. A visit to the Wailing Wall in Jerusalem reveals men's capacity to feel and to cry. David, one of the greatest of all kings, expressed many emotions openly and unashamedly:

> "I am worn out from groaning; all night long I flood my bed with weeping and drench my couch with tears."[9] (Fear of failure)
> "I am worn out calling for help; my throat is parched. My eyes fail, looking for my God."[10] (Helplessness)
> "May those who seek my life be put to shame and confusion. May all who desire my ruin be turned back in disgrace. May those who say to me, 'Aha! Aha!' turn back because of their shame."[11] (Anger)
> "Do not cast me away when I am old; do not forsake me when my strength is gone."[12] (Fear of old age)

No person can cut out or deny part of himself or herself and be integrated. Both male and female must use both parts of their nature—masculine and feminine—otherwise the unused part will atrophy. In New Zealand I was given a gift. It was a strange-looking stuffed bird indigenous to that lovely country. It is the national bird and called a kiwi. It is the size of a small hen, has a long beak, no tail and only a trace of wings. It looks unbalanced.

New Zealanders, who call themselves "kiwis" after this bird, believe that a long time ago the kiwi migrated to their islands as a normal bird with normal, usable wings. But there were no predators of the bird, and therefore it never had to escape by flight, by using its wings. Its wings, therefore, became weaker and smaller through lack of use. The oft-used object lesson in homes, schools and churches "down under" is, "What you don't use, you lose."

So it is with the beautiful character gifts which have been given to men and women. Husband is taught much more than wife not to use the gentler parts of his nature. And as the world shouts at him to deny that part of himself, wife must provide and encourage an atmosphere where he can use all of his characteristics. The rewards will be immeasureable. He will become the kind of father each child, whether boy or girl, needs for a model. He will be the caring, loving, gentle, sensitive, "manly" husband every woman desires. *Tell me what makes a man laugh and I will tell you about his charms. Tell me what makes a man cry and I will tell you about his character.*

Chapter 6

Husbands: Their Cycles, Moods and Rhythms

There is a time for everything, and a season for every activity under heaven . . .

Ecclesiastes

Bob stopped by to pick up a book. He was a college student, a Physical Education major, and he came by often "just to touch base." On this stop-by, he followed me into our son's bedroom which I euphemistically call my office. Organized disorganization lay spread before us: books, papers, files, and notes all over the desk, table, bed and floor. He asked hesitantly, "What's all this . . .?"

"Mess about?" I filled in.

He blushed. "Yeh, what are ya doing?"

"Don't be embarrassed. It is a mess! I am writing a book," I explained.

"Gee, you write? What about?" Embarrassment changed to curiosity.

I told him of my particular interest in a subject about which little was known, but which is beginning to receive attention in sophisticated medical circles. The subject was that of cycles and rhythms in men. I explained that though I did not have much concrete evidence, I had a strong conviction that males, too, have those times whether daily, weekly or monthly, when they feel up or down and either on top of things or depressed.

"Bob," I continued, "we live in an ordered universe of rhythms. The animal kingdom is replete with examples. I do not believe half of the human population is exempt; that is, the male half.

"It took years for scientists and doctors to validate, for instance, that a woman suffered depression around her menstrual time. It took even longer for them to believe that a woman going through the menopause had real, not imagined, symptoms. Finally they found a way to treat some of the symptoms and give a degree of comfort and relief. In time I believe cycles and rhythms will also be validated in men as well, and methods found to treat uncomfortable and adverse symptoms."

I watched Bob as he carefully absorbed everything I was saying. "Doesn't it make sense that it's all right for men to get up tight and emotional, or down, or whatever, just as it is for women? Why can't men have their 'time of the month,' too? Times when they can be allowed to not have it all together, and let their feelings show through. They sometimes have days when the whole world "smells like kerosene," or so some have told me."

As I said this to Bob, his face lit up. "Wow! Do you mean it is O.K. for me, a man, to have down days too, like my girlfriend? I've been tough on myself. For a week or so I go along great. I get up in the morning feeling I can tackle and do anything. Then for three or four days in a row I get so depressed I don't want to get out of bed," he said with what seemed to be excited awareness.

I questioned him further. "How often do you have these down days? Is there any regularity to them?" I asked.

"I can't be sure, but about every ten days or so. Now that I think about it some of my friends experience this too, though they are hesitant to talk about it," he volunteered.

"I don't know, Bob, if this means that you are going through some regular kind of cycle or whatever. But when you feel down, please don't make it worse by coming down on yourself. Because you are male does not exempt you from the privilege of acknowledging that you are human. Honor that humanity. Accept yourself and get off your back!" I pleaded.

With a "Wow—what a relief!" and "See ya!" he went out the door and whistled on the way to his car.

This little encounter and discussion does not prove anything scientifically about the question of cycles and rhythms in men. However it does point up that, if they do exist, men have been culturized to ignore them or deny any such phenomenon. Before pursuing the possibilities that cycles and rhythms might exist, it would be good to look at some definitions:

Rhythm: any kind of movement characterized by the regular recurrence of strong and weak elements.

Cycle: a time interval in which a characteristic, especially a regularly repeated event or sequence of events, occurs; or a single complete execution of a periodically repeated phenomenon; or a periodically repeated sequence of events.

Season: any period of time or one of the four equal natural divisions of the year: spring, summer, autumn, and winter.

Time: a nonspatial continuum in which events occur, a suitable or opportune moment or season.[1]

From these definitions we can see that times and seasons are generalities. Rhythms and cycles are more specific.

Everyone is familiar with the hydrological cycle. Moisture is evaporated from the ocean by the sun, reformed into clouds which circle the planet, and then released in the form of rain or snow. The water sustains vegetation for man and animals to eat, and drains into the sub-strata which provides drinking water. Excess water runs into tributaries and rivers which drain into the ocean. Then the sun heats the ocean and the cycle begins again.

Green plants take our waste in the form of carbon monoxide, and, using any light that is available, mix it with water from the atmosphere to produce oxygen in just the right proportions for humans, animals and plants to breathe. Think of the other cycles in nature. Day and night and the seasons follow each other with inevitable regularity. The tides continually ebb and flow. The night sky reveals the phases of the moon and the movement of the planets around the sun. In wildlife the migrating habits to feed and breed are astounding. North American caribou travel 700 miles along regular routes between tundra breeding grounds and their winter home. Salmon migrate thousands of miles from salt water to fresh, against the wild rapids upstream, to spawn every spring.[2]

Ann Guilfoyle and Edward Ricciuti have observed nature's dependence on cycles for balance. "In nature's world, time and the seasons cycle forever. Days and nights. Springs, summers, autumns, winters. So, too, do the earth's creatures move through the intimate cycles of birth, mating, death. Populations expand and decline. Rest alternates with activity. Cycles within cycles, independent yet interacting. . . The manner in which natural cycles mesh is complex beyond our understanding. Clearly, however, the complexity of nature is not chaotic, but profoundly ordered, so that all parts work together to maintain an equilibrium. Thus balanced, undisturbed by humanity, nature is truly a kingdom at peace."[3]

We humans have our cycles, too. The one which most of us are aware of is the general human cycle of life. We are born. We develop through adolescence to a peak of maturity when we realize our full potentialities. As we grow older, our strength and bodily processes wane, our vital processes stop, and we die.

The most specific human cycle about which we all know, and about which there is considerable information and research, is the twenty-eight day cycle of the female. This is the easiest of human cycles to chart since it is a regular, universal, physical phenomenon which happens to women and which begins at about age twelve.

Unfortunately, many wrong assumptions were drawn about the menstrual cycle or "period" by behaviorists and physicians. As late as 1972 a *New York Times* article quoted a surgeon who said that women were unfit for top jobs because of "the raging hormonal influences" of the menstrual cycle. Endocrinologist Estelle Ramey shot back an answer to the *Times* in a publication in which she announced, "They (men) have them, too, you know."[4] Unfortunately her studies, though respected, were inconclusive. But she firmly believes in the presence of rhythms in men, similar to those in women. Do men have monthly cycles like women? According to Dr. Ramey, professor at Georgetown University Medical School, "Men do have monthly cycles. The evidence of them may be less dramatic, but the monthly changes are no less real."

She describes a sixteen-year study conducted in Denmark in which male urine was tested for the fluctuating amounts of male sex hormones it contained. The result: a pronounced thirty-day rhythm was revealed through the ebb and flow of hormones. Her opinion is that men respond to their cycles in a way that is a fuction of their "culturally acquired self-image. They deny it." This is a fact to be lamented, for it is no doubt the reason the largely male scientific community has not drawn on the information about biological rhythms for the treatment of disease or for protection against disease. Dr. Ramey says, "Menopause in men has been studied somewhat more than the effects of their monthly cycles, but not enough."[5]

At long last, medical science is paying more attention to this issue. Some researchers have even gone so far as to suggest that "the idea that both males and females have cycles and moods, which are associated with certain biological rhythms, is far from nonsense."[6] But, as Dr. Ramey stated, cycles have not been studied nearly enough because of the culturally induced denial of the male against anything "female" happening to him.

One of my dearest friends, a gentle, caring physician-surgeon in his mid-forties, for whom I have profound respect, reacted hostilely when I gave him this chapter of my book to read before its publication. "You demasculinize us when you present the idea that men have rhythms, or cycles, or anything resembling 'periods.' This is the epitome of female castration of the male which you say you are writing against!" Men have not wanted to be tarred with the "negatives" usually associated with the woman's period. However, biological cycles and psychological moods are beginning to be studied as separate, though related, entities. Researchers are discovering that some women have positive moods during and after the menstrual cycle. This should take some of the stigma off the entire concept about the possibility of male cycles and hasten serious study into the matter. Below are brief summations of some of the studies which have been conducted, and validated, on both men and women in body rhythms and cycles.

For several years, sleep investigators have been

familiar with ninety-minute sleep cycles in which neu-
ronal activity erupts in the brain and seems to be responsible for bizarre dreams. More recently they have
discovered that these cycles are present while we are
awake. They are divided into peaks and troughs every
forty-five minutes. These cycles may help explain
such phenomena as mental blocks in memory, and
high creative ability followed by temporary "burn-
out." In males, the penis becomes more tumescent an
average of every ninety minutes. This is usually accompanied by fantasies, sometimes sexual.[7]

Our respiration, blood pressure and heart beat rise
and fall in a cyclical pattern. "Normal" body tempera-
ture varies several degrees a day. This reflects a shift
in a metabolism which has daily cycles. Blood chemistry, blood sugar, hormone levels and urine production have rhythmic patterns. Skin continually replaces
itself. Dead cells are replaced by new ones.

Non-chemical, non-physical processes fluctuate as
well: the keenness of sense, mental alertness, resistance to stress, and moods. These observations are
from studies on both women and men.[8]

The fluctuations that we experience in our bodily
processes are measured by "inner" clocks designed
for the benefit of our personal health and well-being.
The "inner" clock is quite unlike the clock-on-the-wall
designed, so it seems, to imprison us by its sociologi-
cally scheduled dictates.

A psychologist who generously gave of his time to
help in my project, did a study at an emergency hot
line in a medical center. It was his responsibility to
minister to the callers, either by telephone or in the

hospital should they be admitted as patients. Between 1966 and 1970 he spent thousands of hours in this large center. A careful, detailed record was kept of all incoming calls on the hot line. It involved attempted suicides, homicides, rapes, deep depressions, loneliness, premeditated violence, and other depraved human conditions of the psyche. Interestingly, such emergency calls tripled and quadrupled during the full phase of the moon.

Dr. Donald R. Forden, Co-director of the Bakersfield Counseling Group of Bakersfield, said, "When I was in my clinical training at Long Beach Memorial Medical Center in Long Beach, California, in 1970, a computer analysis study was completed. The chairman of the Pastoral Care Department had totaled all the calls for the three previous years coming into the 24-hour Crisis Intervention Hot Line, the calls into the counseling center of the hospital, and the number of people coming into the emergency room. His correlation showed that there was a very noticeable increase in all the calls on the nights of the full moon."[9] So it appears that lunar rhythms very definitely affect psychological balance in human beings.

It is interesting that the female's menstrual cycle coincides with the lunar month which is 29 and ½ days. Human gestation takes nine lunar months. A Miami psychiatrist believes since we are 80 percent water and 20 percent solids, the gravitational force of the moon exerts an influence on the human body, as it does on the ocean waters and tides of our planet.[10]

Another clinical psychiatrist, after his study of 6,000 case histories concludes that "most of our mood swings are the result of altered body chemistry set in motion by our genes and major life stresses."[11] But, he does not rule out the possibility of lunar cycles affecting our behavior and our moodswings.

Much progress has been made in the treatment of emotional, psychological and pathological disturbances due to chemical imbalance. Mood-swings, depressions, and cycles occur in all humans—*both male and female*. President Abraham Lincoln was well-known for deep depressions which were "recurrent and intrinsic, indicating some chemical vulnerability." One of his best-known lows coincided with the breaking of his engagement with Mary Todd. For a week he became reclusive, and some feared he was becoming suicidal. Years later, in an elated state, he engaged in the famous Lincoln-Douglas debates. "Even though Lincoln lost this crucial Senate race, he remained in good spirits. . . In some instances, Lincoln's depressions may have been precipitated by stress, but more often than not they seem to have occurred independently of loss and adversity, as most chemical or metabolic depressions do."[12]

Back in 1931, an industrial psychologist, Rex Hersey, did a study on mood cycles in men. He interviewed industrial workers four times daily during the course of a year. When the data for each week was graphed, there were clear cycles in the moods of almost every man. They varied from three and a half to nine weeks, but they were constant and predictable for each man. Though his work was, in the minds of modern psychologists, "unsophisticated," it was a landmark to begin to acknowledge that men, too, are subject to cycles and moods.[13]

A study by an experimental psychologist in human cycles revealed interesting observations about men's cycles: ". . . the study . . . does not attempt to answer the complicated questions of cause and effect; instead it provides some of the first solid evidence for the existence of cycles in men. I found recurring fluctuations in moods, as measured by various questionnaires, over a three-month period. The length of the cycles varied considerably from man to man and from mood to mood. One subject, for instance, had seven-day cycles for a number of feelings, including elation, anger, and anxiety. Another had varying cycles for different moods that ranged from seven days for anger-hostility to ninety for depression-dejection. In all, I studied variations in a total of 200 mood states for the three months . . . and found a repeating pattern of fluctuation in 120 of the mood states, or 60 percent."[14]

Biologists, too, have been studying infradian (longer than 24 hours) rhythms in men for some time, although most of the important work has been in other countries. "Using various techniques to assess hormone levels they have found clear evidence of testosterone cycles in adult men. The length of the cycles varies among individuals (from five to thirty days) and not all men exhibit a cycle (between half and two-thirds do)."[15]

A Stanford research team found identifiable cycles in testosterone levels ranging in length from 3 to 30 days. They found no correlation between hormone levels and daily moods. "The only association between the two was a correlation between average values for testosterone and depression: men with high levels of the male hormone tended to be more depressed than those with lower levels."[16]

After reading some research by the well-known endocrinologist, Dr. Richard Spark, I picked up the telephone and tried to call him at the Boston Beth Israel Hospital. Unfortunately, he was gone for the day. But the receptionist suggested I might want to speak with one of his close assistants, Dr. Robert A. White, who helped on the research in the article. With my assent, she put him on the line.

He was surprised, even delighted, at my interest in men's cycles. I carefully explained some of the things I had learned. I asked whether there was any validation for them, and did he know of anything new in the field? He agreed with my assertion that if men could understand and acknowledge that they, too, have cycles and varying moods, it would help them understand themselves. It could be freeing and certainly could reduce stress.

I asked him: "Dr. White, would you or your other team assistants be surprised if, indeed, you or someone else were to discover a regular cycle for men, correspondent to that of women?" I wrote down quickly both my questions and his answers.

"Not at all!" he answered emphatically. "We have come upon some interesting findings, now that the question is being asked seriously. Some months ago a student presented a convincing paper on this subject of cycles in men to students who were specializing in endocrinology."

"What was their reaction?" I asked.

"Mixed," he answered. "But the presentation provoked a good deal of discussion and interest. It is now a wide-open subject. I think, in time, the premise will be validated."

My gynecologist gave me some "off-the-cuff" observations when I pressed him about the matter. "It is so nice for me to talk with someone about my ups and downs who does not think I am less husband, or man, or good physician because I admit to this. It is high time someone took an interest in this part of our make-up. We men, like you women, need to admit to moods, depression and times when we want to go and hide. I promise you, if we did, there would be a lot fewer heart attacks in our species!"

A member of my husband's staff dropped into the office while I was there one day. This man, in his late thirties, is as easy going and adaptable as anyone can be. When he was ready to leave, I asked, "Mike, would you be insulted if your wife, or sister, or someone close to you asked, 'What's wrong with you? Are you having your period?' " He sat down, leaned way back, stretched his long legs, and laughed hilariously.

"My wife tells me that about once a month. You bet, whatever you call it, I'm having something. I didn't know much about periods and moods until I got married. Then I began to notice my wife's moods periodically. She became very quiet and tense, sometimes tearful. After a few days it would pass. I'd leave her alone, all to herself," he laughed. "I'd try to support her, do nice things for her, and let her know I understood. I'd think to myself, 'I'd like to have a day or two all to myself sometime!'

"In the past several years I've begun to get 'off-days' every three or four weeks. I'm uptight first thing in the morning before my wife or the children are up, so it isn't my wife or my kids—we're not on each other's case! At first I couldn't understand what was wrong. Why couldn't I cope? Nothing unusual had happened. I'd slept well. But if anyone said or did anything slightly out of 'sync' I came apart, and I didn't know why!" He laughed again and continued. "That day alone, all to myself, which I wished I could have, I now have at least once a month. Sometimes I need two or three days. I am a monster to be around. So my wife takes the car keys, bundles up the kids to take to grandma's, calls a friend for lunch, kisses me good-bye, grins and says, 'Enjoy your period, dear.'

"I don't know that I enjoy the way I feel at those times. I do enjoy being alone for a few hours. And more, I enjoy the understanding which has come into our relationship, minus the friction we had had before. We know now that there are times when both husband and wife experience cycles of psychological, physiological 'downs.' And what's more, I don't feel any less of a man because of it!"

When men are able to accept the possibility of cycles and rhythms in their own lives, they will be better able to adapt to the times and seasons of life.

"There is a time for everything, and a season for
    every activity under heaven:
a time to be born and a time to die,
a time to plant and a time to uproot,
a time to kill and a time to heal,

a time to tear down and a time to build,
a time to weep and a time to laugh,
a time to mourn and a time to dance,
a time to scatter stones and a time to gather them,
a time to embrace and a time to refrain,
a time to search and a time to give up,
a time to keep and a time to throw away,
a time to tear and a time to mend,
a time to be silent and a time to speak,
a time to love and a time to hate,
a time for war and a time for peace."[17]

For everything—for everyone—there is a time and a season. I believe that includes cycles, moods and rhythms—times and seasons—for species *husband!*

Chapter 7

Husbands: Within a Dark Wood

In the middle of our life, I came to myself within a dark wood where the straight way was lost. Ah, how hard it is to tell of that wood, savage and harsh and dense. So bitter is it that death is hardly more.

Dante Alighieri

When our daughter Julie was twelve, I watched her one day as she was engaged in a deep discussion with her daddy. They talked about girls and boys, and growing up. And, her daddy asked her, as every child in the world is asked at some time, "What are you going to be when you grow up, honey?" After many thoughtful moments, Julie listed several things which appealed to her. Together daddy and daughter explored the possibilities. Then, mischievously, she looked up at her daddy and asked, "What are you going to be when you grow up, Daddy?"

Though Julie was teasing, her question is more profound than clever. As both her dad and mom grow through the middle years of life, we continue to learn

77

more of its profundity. Until recently, folk wisdom projected the notion that one stopped "growing" after marriage. A husband and wife, a father and mother *were*. It was assumed everything that needed to be known was automatically known until you died. Old people were either lovable or irascible—mostly the latter—to the young who did not understand them, but few challenged their maturity or dared to suggest that longevity in and of itself did not negate the need or ability to grow.

Since the 1930's we have learned a great deal about growing. Children develop through usually predictable stages: infancy, childhood, pubescence and adolescence. After that they fumble their way through to young adulthood. In the past thirty years considerable attention has also focused on the elderly. Terms like senior citizen, older adulthood, retired persons, plus college courses in geriatrics have given them a semblance of purposeful personhood.

Rather than suspending himself between youth and old age, a man named Walter Pitkin wrote a book called *Life Begins at Forty*. Fifty years ago he had meager knowledge about physiological and psychological phenomena concerning life at age forty, especially in the male. Only the title caught on. It translated itself into "go to it while you have it." It issued forth the phrase, "the fiery forties." This fragmentary bit of soliloquy caused many a wife to wonder if she would do both herself and her spouse a favor by putting him in "solitary" until he reached the age of fifty.

What emerged, therefore, was a good deal of understanding about youth and older adulthood, but minimal awareness of the problems and potentialities of mid-life. Little research was done on the so-called middle years for two major reasons. First, it was not until the middle of this century that people began to live through the middle years. In 1900 a small percent of the population was "middle-aged." A man's life expectancy was forty-eight and a woman's fifty-one.[1]

Another reason the middle years were ignored is that ours has been a youth-oriented culture propagandized by Madison Avenue and television. We are urged to use "Erase-the-Wrinkle" formula, "longer-lasting" deodorant, and "tiger-eyes" mascara. If we will only avail ourselves of face lifts and hair transplants, the Fountain of Youth will be ours forever. Or so the sales pitch goes.

Beyond statistics—marriage and divorce, illness and health, life expectancy, occupation and income—little was known about the middle stage of life. Though the average age of the adult work force is now forty-five, and life expectancy is seventy or more, most people arrive there by trial and error. Happily, that is changing! For the first time in our history we are becoming not a youthful, but a mature society. Sociologists are recognizing the enormous diversity between the middle-aged and the elderly. We are discovering that middle life—and beyond!—can be successful, positive experiences.

One of our happier and more helpful discoveries has been that there is developmental transition and order in the adult years. We are more than young organisms suddenly grown old, who sit and wait for the undertaker. Slowly, but surely, these transitions and struggles are becoming less difficult to understand and experience.

In a later chapter I discuss briefly the transitional stages through which young men metamorphose into early adulthood. Dr. Daniel Levinson, who did much of the original research on what he calls "The Seasons of a Man's Life," has this to say about the middle years: "I felt intuitively that the years around age 40 have a special importance in a person's life ... I decided to focus on the decade from age 35 to 45. During this 'mid-life decade,' I reasoned, one made the shift from 'youth' to 'middle age.' "[2]

Dr. Levinson defines "young" and "old" as archetypal symbols with many meanings. "... 'young' represents birth, growth, possibility, initiation, openness, energy, potential ... Conversely, 'old' is a symbol representing termination, fruition, stability, structure, completion, death." What about "middle age"? Perhaps the best description of "Mid-Life Transition" is that supplied by Levinson. It is the developmental period which confronts "the Young and Old within oneself and seeks new ways of being Young/Old."[3]

It is extremely important for both husband and wife to learn some of the dynamics of the middle years—"the dark wood"—of the diminishing species known as *husband*.

Middle age, the "change of life," and its accompanying symptoms, used to be the strict domain of females only. Those with the menstrual cycle. Something like the private "snooty" women's colleges. Guess what! Most women's private colleges have gone co-ed, and so has "change of life!" Like it or not, it happens to husband and wife.

Raymond Hull, teacher, lecturer, and author, and Dr. Helmut Ruebsaat, M.D., have together expressed in their book, *The Male Climacteric*, how important it is for men to accept the major turning point of middle age and its changes. "Only recently has discussion of a male change of life been removed from the mass media list of taboo subjects. So many men between the ages of forty-five and sixty are undergoing major physical and emotional changes which produce severe disruptions in their health, careers and private lives—as well as in their general societal behavior—the subject can no longer be ignored.

"It's not simply a question of sudden chills or momentary lapse of memory, although these can be humiliating if they occur at inconvenient times. Climacteric symptoms, whether cyclical or indefinitely persistent, can have far-reaching effects.

"An executive decision may be based on emotional reactions; a politician may be forced to make policy judgments at a time of temporary loss of mental acuity; a father may disrupt his family's home life in pursuit of illusive and unrealistic dreams of youth. It is time that we openly acknowledge the existence of the climacteric, in order to deal realistically with the very serious problems it can cause.[4]

A man looks at himself in the mirror as he begins to go through his morning hygiene routine. For the first time he sees not one or two gray hairs, but handfuls. His skin hangs saggy and wrinkled under his chin. He stoops over to put on his socks and comes up breathing with difficulty. He remembers that he dropped most of the balls Junior threw out at him the previous afternoon. As he fastens his trousers they feel unusually tight. The belt around his middle rejects the notch beside the buckle imprint. He moves to the next notch. He recalls his inability to make love to his wife the night before. A wave of unexplainable emotion blankets him. The man is in deep grief. Grief indicates loss—of a person, of a sentimental memento, of a place, of a stage of life. This man is grieving for the loss of youth.

One such voyager, Jim Conway, put it this way: "My depression had grown all through the spring, summer, and fall. By October it had reached giant proportions. I would often stare out the window or simply sit in a chair, gazing into space. . . Repeatedly I had fantasies of getting on a sailboat and sailing off to some unknown destination where no one knew me and where I carried no responsibility for anyone in my church or my family. On a cold wintry night, I went for a long walk and made some decisions. I would resign as pastor of the church . . . drop my doctoral program . . . I would no longer be writing. I would also legally turn everything over to Sally, take only our 1968 Cutlass, and start driving south. For me, it was all over."[5]

Ages ten, twenty and thirty come as exciting stepping stones to life's dreams and the pot of gold at the end of the rainbow. Seventy, eighty and ninety stand as milestones to triumph of the soul, spirit and body. But forty, fifty and sixty can feel like millstones around the neck. Middle age! Someone who must have had intimate knowledge of this "passage" of life declared, "Middle age is the cruelest joke life plays on a man."[6] The man in the mirror observing himself seems to have lost his youth suddenly. However, what is happening to him is less a crisis than it is a process. He is in transition. He is experiencing a "passage" of life variously described as the mid-life crisis, male climacteric (a turning point in human life), menopause (the pause between stages of life), middlescense, *male menopause*.

As recently as ten years ago, this latter term was emphatically denied application to men. The Greek word *menos* means a month, as in the case of the woman's monthly menstrual cycle. Since men do not menstruate, it was deemed inappropriate to think of them as experiencing a cessation of this occurance. Perhaps a better term will emerge, but the phrase *male menopause* is gaining respect from psychologists, psychiatrists, and physicians for solid reasons. For example, as life moves on, women decrease in estrogen output and finally cease producing it entirely at the end of the menopausal years. On the other hand, the male hormone, testosterone, does not change dramatically and rapidly in men. Unless there is a pathological problem, testosterone levels usually remain within the normal adult range throughout old age. However, attention is now being given to recently discovered "free" testosterone in the blood. This is testosterone which is not bound to protein and is "active." This so-called free testosterone does show a marked decline with age. As this occurs, symptoms similar to those in menopausal women begin to appear.

Dr. Robert H. Williams describes these symptoms: "In addition to experiencing the hot flashes, approximately half of these patients experience increased irritability, inability to concentrate, episodes of depression, etc., and libido and sexual potential invariably decreases. This entity has been designated the 'male climacteric.' "[7]

Men and women, husbands and wives, have many things in common in middle age. Thus, to know about each other is to know about oneself. An empathetic viewing of female menopause can teach men about their own physiological and psychological problems, needs and mysteries during this stage of life.

Menopause, though not easy for many women, is traumatic for men. For one thing, men cannot use physiological changes as a rationale, because there are no overt symptoms. Also, male pride and "machismo" prevent men from admitting that "something" is happening to them. After all, they are men! They are supposed to be able to handle anything that comes along. So says society. Yet, Dr. Peter L. Brill, Director of the Center for the Study of Adult Development at the Hospital of the University of Pennsylvania, says: "Eighty percent of all American males will experience a moderate to severe crisis around the age of forty, or in mid-life, so it's important that men learn to understand this phenomenon so it may become a positive event in their lives."[9] Some men will dismiss the matter with an offhanded, "My father never went through this." In all probability his father did but endured silently, because he wasn't supposed to talk about it.

It is precisely in this area of transition and potential difficulty that the "chauvinized male syndrome", described earlier, manifests itself. What a tragedy! At a time when a man needs at least as much understanding as a woman, because there are no detectable physical reasons for the strange, inexplicable things which are happening to him, he insulates himself from those who love him, sometimes from the world, and begins his journey into a long, lonely "dark wood."

At what age does this coming to oneself "within a dark wood" begin? Dante Alighieri began his struggling in the black forest at age thirty-seven, and wrote the poignant strophes quoted at the beginning of this chapter at age forty-two. Dr. Theodore Rubin, M.D., psychoanalyst, observes that it can occur between the ages of thirty-five and fifty-five, but it can also occur at age sixty or later and sometimes in the early thirties.[10] Dr. Daniel Levinson, Professor of Psychology at Yale University, places the center of this critical male middlelife transition at about age forty,[11] as mentioned above. Dr. William A. Nolen, M.D., a practicing physician and author, recalls his first-hand experience with male menopause just before his fifty-first birthday.[12]

How long will this transition period last? Dr. Nolen states that it will last anywhere from three to twelve months. Hull and Ruebsaat, authors of *The Male Climacteric*, journeyed "within the wood" for five years. Other men wander in and out of the dark mazes for twenty years. Some symptoms show up for a short time and disappear. Then along come other disturbing signs signifying other phases. It is extremely important to understand, however, that this crisis of a man's life will, like all crises, eventually pass.

Women are learning how to cope because they know what is happening to them. But most men are not aware that they are in a change-of-life transition. Coping is, therefore, often supplanted by subconscious compensatory behavior. For nearly eighteen months I had not seen a couple who are casual friends of ours. When at a community concert they suddenly reappeared, I did not recognize the husband. He wore a bright orange sports jacket, plaid slacks, an expensive ruffled shirt with orange embroidery and tan mirror-shiny shoes with see-through plastic heels. I never notice shoes, but these emanated such sparkle they could not not be noticed.

Now, I think it is high time men got out of grays, browns and blacks, but even for my expansive tastes this was a bit much. Topping it off was one of the highest, curliest, fuzziest, "naturals" ever perpetrated on the protein called hair!

To make matters worse, he insisted on answering my "How are you?" for the next forty-five minutes. I certainly found out! He was all right, but everything and everyone around him was all wrong. Not until later did I realize how profoundly the trauma of middle life was affecting this man. Everything about him shouted out his hurt, anxiety, bewilderment, frustration and I-will-show-everybody-that-I-am-not-getting-old attitude.

I still see him occasionally. The colors are not quite so bright. The hair not quite so curly. The bravado not quite so compulsive. Some acceptance has taken place. The "Peter Pan" within him is making peace with the wonderful mature man he is becoming. In a youth oriented culture, aging is not easy. But becoming older and eventually being old is a whole lot better than easy acquiescence to the alternative! Even to the most faith filled person, dying isn't that great!

What are some of the physical symptoms of male menopause?

Urinary irregularities Urinary flow may be disturbed at the climacteric due to enlargement of the prostate gland, which is probably due to hormonal changes. An increased need to urinate, perhaps up to eight or ten times a day.

Fluid retention Water accumulates in body tissues, especially in the extremities—the feet and hands—causing swelling.

Hot flashes The face feels flushed from a few seconds to a few hours, accompanied by sweating and then chills, or unusual flow of perspiration.

Heart symptoms A man hears his heart pounding while lying in bed. The heartbeat at times may be irregular.

Pseudoangina Sharp pain in the front center of his chest or on the left side. Pseudoangina is brought on by anxiety, not by any heart defect. (However, any such continued irregularity should be reported to your physician.)

Peptic ulcers Middle-aged men are a high-risk group

for ulcers of the esophagus, stomach and duodenum, because of excessive production of hydrochloric acid in the stomach. Nausea is also common.

Itching Disturbances of the autonomic nervous system cause itching which feels like insects crawling on the skin, or there may be stinging sensations.

Air hunger Sometimes an anxious climacteric male becomes tensely aware of his own breathing. He panics for more air, and deepens his breathing. He may feel that he is suffocating. Air hunger differs from shortness of breath and is accompanied by puffing and panting, noticed by observers.

Liver spots These have nothing to do with disease of the liver, but sometimes come in the middle years due to changing skin pigmentation.

Headaches Some men never experience these until mid-life and then, due to hormonal disturbances, stress or emotional tension, have them frequently.

Dizziness The man feels as if he is about to lose his balance. It is much like the faintness after suddenly standing up, but this type of dizziness is not produced by sudden movement. It can come on when a man is walking or sitting still. Sometimes he comes close to losing consciousness. He has to stop whatever he is doing and cling to something. This is usually a vasomotor effect, caused by a disturbance of the blood flow.[13]

It is during this season of the man, that women must be prepared to extend at least as much empathy as they hope to receive during their menopause. The truth is, women have much more going for them than men do: (1) It is okay for women to have menopause.

But, it is still considered "unmasculine" and "demeaning" for men to have "female" physiological phenomena. (2) Though there is yet much to be learned about female menopause, there is a good deal of knowledge and information available about cause, symptoms and treatment. Estrogen replacement therapy cautiously used is a gift from heaven, literally! However, to date, hormonal replacement for men has proved unsuccessful, inefficient, and, perhaps detrimental. (3) Because of cultural and sociological mores, women can air their feelings. They can get depressed; they can get emotional; they can laugh one moment and cry the next; they can joke about the nuisance of "hot flashes"; they can dash to the medicine cabinet for estrogen pills, or to the doctor for a shot. They have these privileges because they are female.

Let a husband try any or all of the above, and wives, children, and friends may feel the urge to get him to the nearest psychiatrist. It is grossly unfair, and it is time to allow men, husbands, to be human. It is time to acknowledge the double difficulties they endure during their middle years.

Dr. Nolen shares of his experiences with men going through this difficult time. "Looking back on my life as a physician, I now realize that many of the men I have treated at one time or another were in the throes of the male menopause. I didn't make the diagnosis at the time because I didn't know, until I was afflicted myself, that there was any such condition. Even now it isn't mentioned in most medical textbooks, and there are many doctors—most of them under 55— who deny the condition exists. I can assure them that it does exist, and that the man in that situation needs all the help he can get."[14]

What are some of the psychological problems of male menopause?

Accepting mortality One of the more awesome and frightening aspects is that a husband is suddenly confronted with his mortality. During these mid-years he falls well below his earlier attainments of functioning, both physically and sometimes mentally. He runs slower while trying to keep up with Junior. He cannot do without those extra hours of sleep. Or, conversely, he has trouble getting sufficient sleep. His vision, coordination and hearing are less acute. He is more prone to dwell on his physical well-being than at any other time in his life. He may think any ache, pain or impairment may become permanent and lead to death. He might continue to wish for immortality, but he now becomes more realistic about what he will do with the rest of his life.

"Whatever else happens during these years, the mid-life syndrome develops as a spiritual crisis. For the first time, the middlescent lives life between sunrise and sunset. He numbers his years not in terms of birth but of death. Instead of marching forward from birthday to birthday, he looks at the number of years until death-day. In the middle years we are shaken by the reality that we are finite and mortal."[15]

Career goals Many of a man's life dreams and ambitions remain unrealized when he hits mid-life. He begins to face the fact that he will not become an executive in his union or corporation. Or, if he owns a small business, he will never be rich. His dreams of a beautiful home, expensive car and travel to exotic places have not been, nor may ever be realized.

He turns inward to discover he is Mr. Average Citizen, and that his goals and dreams for himself probably were unrealistic. Some husbands who are "successful" financially or status-wise may spend the middle years acknowledging how little their success means to them.

"Every man in the Mid-life Transition starts to see that the hero of the fairy tale does not enter a life of eternal, simple happiness . . . (and begins) to grieve and accept the symbolic death of the youthful hero within himself."[16]

Meaning in life A man in the mid-life transitions may be so oppressed and beaten down in the struggle for survival that there is no energy or will left to give life meaning. He withdraws from his work and home and turns inward. He merely exists. It is during these crucial years that he may turn to alcohol or affairs with younger women. He may experience meaninglessness to the point of his own subconscious death wish, and be killed in an accident.

Or he may opt for a more constructive alternative. He may decide to give up the frenzied clock-oriented urban corporate rat race for a little restaurant or grocery store in a rural town. He may build a boat with life's minimal necessities and take to the open sea. He may learn a new trade, and use his hands as well as his mind, and completely change his lifestyle.

A clergyman of a small church decided, upon turning fifty, to take a year's sabbatical at a time which seemed inappropriate because his parish was just beginning to expand and grow. But was it inappropriate? Not for him. He had his priorities in order. To their credit his congregation supported his decision.

His legacy It is this time in life when a husband who has faced the realization of mortality feels the need to pass on something worthy to future generations. This may include material possessions, enterprises, arranging a financial start for his progeny. He may work for a service club to become "Man of the Year." He may chair community projects, charitable institutions and colleges. He needs to believe he has given something of himself to something enduring. This altruism is, in part, a vehicle of the search and claim for immortality.

He becomes intensely interested in his children, their spouses and especially the grandchildren. To the latter he needs to give something of himself: affection, joy, laughter, little "no-no's" on the sly, advice, trips to Disneyland. To him they signify an extension of himself and his mortality which he now sees more clearly than he did before.

Sexuality An interesting attestation to the crisis of mid-life is found in ancient Israel's King David.[17] The warrior-king, then fifty years old, defeated the Jebusites and declared Jerusalem his capital. He had routed the Edomites, the Moabites and the Ammonites. He had fought and subdued the troublesome Philistines which set the stage for a United Kingdom and the Golden Age of Israel. David, always in the front lines, had led the attack and issued the orders.

One more trouble spot surfaced. The Ammonites and Syrians joined forces in a final attempt to eradi-

cate this motley bunch, led by David, which had con-
quered nearly all of Palestine. At this point, a little
noticed but interesting event is recorded in the story.
"In the spring, at the time when kings go off to war,
David sent Joab out with the king's men and the
whole Israelite army. They destroyed the Ammonites
and besieged Rabbah (the capital city). *But David
remained in Jerusalem*"[18] (italics added for emphasis).

Think of it! The last battle to go. Would not King
David have wanted to be at the head of the Israelite
army to taste, with his commanders and troops, the
delight and exhilaration of final victory? Yet we're
told: "At the time when kings go off to war . . . David
remained in Jerusalem."

Was he preoccupied? Was he battle weary? Did he
take flight from stress? Was he worried about the outcome? Had he lost the magic touch? With all his success had meaning gone out of his life? Were his sexual
powers diminished? Fascinating questions for which
there are no ready answers, but their mere asking
suggests that the mid-life crisis played a larger role in
what happened than has previously been recognized.
And what happened? David remained in Jerusalem in
his palace. He saw Bathsheba and sent for her.

Sexual problems probably throw a man into fear
and panic more than any of the other menopausal
symptoms. His masculinity, his manhood, his male-
ness are more intricately wrapped up in his sexual
abilities than are a woman's. Certain physical things
have to happen before a man can have sex, which is
not the case for a woman. And many, many men
experience a lack of potency temporarily or periodical-

ly, especially in the middle years. Prior to that time, he had sexually been all man. So great had been his sexual prowess in his younger years that the major problem was one of control, not expression. Who could have imagined there would come a moment when he would not be able to "perform" at will. Yet, there does come that moment to virtually every man —every husband.

"The work of William H. Masters, M. D. and Virginia Johnson has made enormous contribution to our knowledge of the physiological changes that occur with advancing age and how they affect our sexual response . . . in short, things slow down a bit with advancing age, but they don't grind to a halt. The slowing of other functions does not produce as much anxiety as change relating to sex. Dr. Masters observed, 'Men are also slower to run around the block, but somehow that doesn't worry us as much. . .' The demand level for both sexes may slowly be reduced over the course of time, even to once every ten days, but continuity is most important. Physicians also advise maintaining a steady sex life as a preventative measure against prostatitis, a chronic painful condition suffered by many older men. Sex is also good exercise, relieving tension and anxiety and increasing feelings of love and self-esteem. It is as vital a need in old age as it is in youth."[19]

Regardless of how much wives try to understand, encourage or empathize, they will never know the utter devastation of what happens to the husband the first time he loses potency. The fright and panic which set in intensify the problem. It is the beginning

HUSBANDS: WITHIN A DARK WOOD / 95

of the decline of the "sex at any time" syndrome, and, of necessity, the beginning of a new relationship between husband and wife. It is, in a sense, the end of an era, which both have taken for granted. It is the beginning of a new one. But, the new era can bring a depth of love that neither partner has previously experienced in their marriage. Wife realizes she no longer can play the "I can have it any time," or "I wish he would leave me alone tonight," or "I am too tired" games. In grand maturity she becomes a true partner and participant in this most intimate of all love expressions. At times, she may be more than a fifty percent partner. She may be fully responsible in sexual love. Together they learn that the joy of loving each other's bodies without concern for orgasmic climax in every sexual union is freeing and beautiful. With wisdom and patience they enter a new and deeper understanding of married sexual love.

"There is nothing more beautiful in the world than the man who resolves his mid-life crisis. He comes out of it with a sense of knowing. He becomes a mentor for others and feels value and potency. He feels an emotional depth that hasn't been there for 20 years."[20] Husband and wife have knowledge they did not have before. They can look ahead with optimism because of wisdom gained in the past. Mid-life gives them a "second wind." Usually, there is some degree of financial freedom. Husband and wife are alone again, without the multitudinous demands of kids. They can begin to bring back into their marriage the excitement of earlier years, without the mistakes.

Mid-life can mean time for short overnights away or

for traveling to the oft-talked-of dream places. Together, they can take up hobbies, college courses,
dancing and a multitude of things for which there
never was time before. Together they have the equipment to make the most out of the second half of life.
They needn't prove anything to anyone. Or please
everyone. They have earned the right to be who they
are.

This potentially difficult time of life for both husband and wife can be a time of giving oneself to a
cause that is larger than daily existence. It can be a
time to deepen the search for meaning, especially in
the spiritual dimension. It can be a time to test one's
faith.

Mid-life years are years of metamorphoses. I am ut-
terly fascinated by the life cycle of the monarch butterfly! Millions of them travel thousands of miles to
winter. As they rendezvous and rest with wings
spread, this kingly species sets ablaze, with brilliant
fiery red, a remote section of jungle in the mountains
of Mexico.

Do any of us know what this little creature goes
through to become, in its gorgeous fragility, endur-
ingly tough? It begins as an egg the size of the head of
a pin. A few days later it emerges as a striped caterpillar which will multiply its original weight by 2700
times—a voracious eater. The larva sheds its skin five
times as it grows. The final shedding occurs when the
fully developed caterpillar stops eating and perches in
a sheltered place. The larva then violently dislodges
its last skin to reveal a chrysalis, or pupa. For several
weeks the pupa hangs quietly, literally by a thread,

while inside it is developing into a full-fledged butterfly.

The time has come for the adult to emerge, and the
chrysalis begins to crack. Gingerly the butterfly frees
itself from its snug temporary home. But what is
"wrong" with it? It looks strange, ugly, wet, and
slimy with wings that are fleshy and limp. This is the
beautiful creature that will fly for thousands of miles?

Then an amazing event takes place. This wet, limp
"thing" reaches out and climbs to a twig for support.
Slowly, it begins to move its wings, little by little. It
fans them to bring life and vitality into the veins—the
support system of the wings. For a prolonged period
this newly born butterfly works and pumps and
pushes and stretches and fans back and forth as
gradually the wings expand and harden. After hours
of tortuous struggle, the adult monarch butterfly,
with wings expanded, soars away to begin a new generation.

An entomologist friend explained how the last pain-
fully slow, struggling process is absolutely necessary
to the survival of the adult. If anything should inter-
vene—a predator, or a fall from its support—the monarch would not gain full maturity and would die. The
pumping, fanning process this amazing insect struggles through toughens it for all that is involved in its
last stage of mature adulthood.

The parallel between the metamorphosis of the
monarch and the transition years between young and
old—the middle years—is striking! It is a time for
shedding the once necessary but restrictive cocoon.

Many books have been written in recent years

about transitional stages of life through which each of us travels. Many books have been written about marriage. In 1955 a book appeared which described succinctly and poetically the transitional stages of married life. In my opinion that little book is still unsurpassed in its beauty, insight, and wisdom. *Gift from the Sea* by Anne Morrow Lindbergh should be required reading for every couple preparing for marriage, and regularly thereafter by husband and wife.

Little was known about the mid-life syndrome in husbands when this little book was written. Yet it is stunningly contemporary. About this phenomenon Mrs. Lindbergh writes, "Perhaps middle age is, or should be, a period of shedding shells; the shell of ambition, the shell of material accumulation and possessions, the shell of the ego. Perhaps one can shed at this stage in life as one sheds in beach living; one's pride, one's false ambitions, one's mask, one's armor . . . Perhaps one can at last in middle age, if not earlier, be completely oneself. And what a liberation that would be!"[21]

Chapter 8

Husbands:
They Also Have
Other Choices

The tissue of the life to be
  We weave with colors all our own,
And in the field of destiny
  We reap as we have sown.

John Greenleaf Whittier

"Alternate lifestyles" is a sophisticated and fashionable phrase. It connotes a grand buffet from which one can choose any number of fancy delights at will. It sounds something like an ice cream store which advertises thirty-one flavors. What ecstasy! To be able to choose out of all those tantalizing possibilities!

All potential husbands have a variety of tantalizing choices before them. There are an array of lifestyles, other than being married, which have gained wide acceptance. This is a new phenomenon which would have been strange and shocking as recently as one generation ago. In the past, boy and girl eventually grew up to become husband and wife. It was, in a sense, manifest destiny. Singleness was almost something of which to be ashamed. The other lifestyles which have become commonplace today virtually did not exist, and if they did, they had not come "out of the closet."

Some call these new lifestyles progress. Other call them moral decay. Just how far have we come? What is different about today's mores? Maybe some of the younger set who read this book do not know that some of today's ways are quite different from those of a few decades ago.

In grandfather's day in the "old country," marriages were arranged by two families who thought that a son and a daughter would make a good match. The families met and discussed the arrangement. Usually a dowry—money, property or cattle—was brought by a prospective bride to a prospective husband. In some cultures, the couple did not meet until the wedding day. This kind of arrangement may be abhorrent to us. But the couple shared respect, friendship, and they learned to love each other. Many of that generation, and those of cultures who still practice this, would tell our young people that those marriages lasted, and they were based on a whole lot more than body chemistry.

How has love and marriage fared in the United States with the practice of a young man and a young woman meeting, falling in love, and the man asking the young woman to marry him? How "happily ever after" do they live?

In the 1920's it was Hollywood that idealized romantic love. Through its outpourings on the silver screen it equated physical attraction with love. In the decades of the twenties through the fifties this idealized concept prevailed. Since then the formula of "chemistry-equals-love-equals-marriage", which results in "living happily ever after," has been perpetuated even with the introduction of alternate life styles. In that past golden era, the concept and dream of romantic love and marriage held up fairly well. Our agrarian society was preoccupied with the Great Depression, and something was needed to make those gloomy years happier. The romanticism of courting, marrying and facing the world together through rain or shine captured the quixotic nature in old and young alike.

There was a certain "mating game" ritual to follow. He and she became sweethearts. They danced at school proms and walked in the moonlight, holding hands. They paired their dreams and they pledged their virginal love. They prepared in blush and innocence for that magic day of bliss—their wedding. In shy wonderment they kissed each other good night and parted, each to go to their own beds and dream of the other. They chose one "flavor" for life. They married and put down roots—that missing something—which many are trying so hard to find now.

Abruptly, so it seemed, the days of nostalgic demureness gave way to paroxysms of scientific eructations and upheaval. Mushroom clouds signaled the end of the "age of innocence." During the term of the "smiling president" of the fifties the world changed irrevocably. Affluence broadened our tastes and desires and sophisticated us. With the advent of planet-destroying weapons, and the mystery of the man-in-the-moon solved once and for all, it was time to get rid of nostalgia, fantasy and idealism. Lovers, who had looked up at a moon which illuminated a universe meant only for them, now sat in the corner of a semidark room. They watched a small square screen as a strangely clad creature set foot on the moon. Their golden evanescent moon-rays were blurred by dusty footprints. Their romantic moonbeams disintegrated into radio beams. Lighter, happy days were at an end.

Away with the old! Bring on the new! A new "cause celebre" was needed to fill the vacuum. Everything old and traditional came under attack. Youth wanted honesty, not hypocrisy. It was rough on their parents and on those who held many things sacred. But it was perhaps needed. Institutions and life patterns went through wrenching and tortuous self-examination and reluctant change.

Though women have made gains in virtually every area, men still are, and still want to be, the primary aggressors in relationships with women whether for temporary involvement or for marriage. Call it ego, masculinity or tradition, if a woman pursues, the man often retreats. What with the invasion of his territory and the pushing back of his wilderness, he clings tenaciously to one of the few remaining institutions—the aggressor "instinct" of the male.

Author Gittelson, quoted earlier, wrote about the male turning away from traditional marriage: "In almost all men . . . the decline of *dominus* (master, once a title of honor accorded to men) on the domestic front was releasing powerful emotions . . . Demoralized, they resigned from once-esteemed male roles. Some of the steadiest husbands were turning slippery as mercury. Some of the fondest fathers were turning into strangers. Family men were turning into playboys. Straights were turning into gays . . . Divorce and separation . . . were increasing everywhere . . . so were the number of delinquent fathers . . . so were the number of husbands battering their wives . . . When dominus was obstructed from its normal channels, it had to erupt into rage."[1]

Let us take a look at some of the choices husbands and potential husbands can make, and see the way these alternate choices may or may not work out in practice.

Singleness

At ages eighteen and twenty, twenty-three percent of males stay single. Between ages twenty to twenty-four, nearly sixty-six percent prefer single bliss. From ages twenty-five to twenty-nine, twenty-eight percent are still single.[2] (It is important to note these figures are the never-marrieds and do not include singles because of divorce.)

Dr. Daniel J. Levinson, noted psychologist and author of the book *The Seasons of a Man's Life*, has mapped a detailed authoritative account of the hidden patterns that shape a man's life. He presents clues about a young man's choice for singleness in western culture. In other cultures young men marry and start families as early as age seventeen. In western culture, however, at age seventeen and for approximately fifteen years thereafter, a young man moves from adolescence to adulthood. Between seventeen and twenty-two, a young man is in pre-adulthood, half in, and half out of boyhood and adulthood. Though at ages eighteen and twenty, seventy-one percent of the male population marry, not many of these marriages will survive. This is a "limited commitment" age, without much self-examination, and with no preparation. Therefore, in this boy-man high marriage age, there is high marriage mortality rate.[3]

The high mortality rate mentioned by Dr. Levinson makes up a high percentage of the singles phenomenon. Over thirty percent of our population is single. A small portion of the thirty percent are widowed or never-marrieds (of marriageable age). The overwhelming majority are divorced. Singles are no longer a subculture. They are a vital, dynamic group of the citizenry. Many businesses have sprung up to accommodate and entice singles—bars, night clubs, discos, travel tours and varying types of get-acquainted enterprises.

A television news show zeroed in on the behavior, the thinking and desires of singles. Many like this lifestyle. There is "something going on every night if you want to keep that busy," one said. Others felt lonely and isolated, especially when they had something they wanted to share with someone. Fathers, who go to the home of their ex-wives, shared how they are saddened "every time we say 'goodby' to the kids." Men seem to be more afraid of meeting someone in case the relationship should develop and "something go wrong again." Many more women than men attend weekend fun retreats. Usually both men and women are looking for the "right person," but that rarely happens.

A psychiatrist on one of the current television programs, who works with singles, believes most of the singles she has observed are generally dissatisfied with being single. She expects a major turnaround on the singles scene in the next few years, and that most persons will again go into traditional marriage lifestyles.

Our recent society has militated against marriage. Business, industry, education and politics override the moral and the economic importance of the family. Industry has moved executives like pawns on a chess board with promise of promotion. This, too, is changing because of career wives. However, frequent change of residence, promise of travel and entertainment, promotion and self-gratification tickle the idealism and fantasy of a young man. Why get tied down when there is so much else to do, to realize and enjoy? One young man in his early twenties who married said, "It takes courage to get married. All of my friends are going to have fun, and settle down in another ten years, maybe."

While their fathers took on immediate responsibility and postponed self-gratification, today's young men reverse the process. They have seen the "trap" their fathers got into, and have learned that dad never had the rainy day for which he was working and saving. Father had a heart attack. So son will have his fun now, and take on responsibility later. In his single state he will have economic prosperity rather than live hand-to-mouth with a wife and babies. Singleness is not confined to young men. Some men choose it for their entire life, and others may choose it after many years of marriage.

Living Together

Another choice is that of living together. With the double standard for women dramatically reduced, and the pill, it is more convenient for a man to live with a woman. Theoretically, there is no responsibility. Sex is available. There is not much fear of pregnancy, and, if it should occur, there is abortion. If one or the other gets tired of the relationship, he or she can leave at will. Though statistics are impossible to obtain on couples living together engaging in sex, it is estimated that there are tens of thousands opting for this lifestyle.

Heartbroken parents watch their daughters or sons in this situation, and do not know how to approve, or bless, or cooperate with this setup. Many couples choose this lifestyle as a trial "marriage." But usually it is doomed to failure, because this kind of relationship theoretically makes no demands and, at the first sign of trouble, the way out is simple and easy. One or the other picks up and leaves.

In any living-together relationship about which I know firsthand, or have heard about from parents, the ending of the story varies little. Most of the time it is the man who leaves the woman. The woman, though she may be a student or a career person, keeps house, does the laundry, helps a man (typing papers, etc.) to get his degree, or get promoted to a better job. Either one who leaves, however, leaves behind a rejected mate who feels worthless. One disillusioned young college student said, "I helped her get her master's degree, and then she split!"

The famous Marvin versus Marvin case involving living-togethers is a landmark. It established a legal precedent after the breakup of an actor and his live-in "wife." She was awarded a healthy sum termed "palimony." Living together without benefit of "that little piece of paper" has become a bonanza for the legal profession. Prenuptial and living-together contracts are drawn up just in case "it doesn't work out."

Bitterness and disillusionment happen after splitting up, just as in marriage. They fight, just as in marriage. Both feel abused, and rejected, just as in marriage. What is not "just as in marriage" is a long word with an even longer meaning: *commitment!* By non-commitment, couples are relieved of any responsibility to bring out the best in the other in a tight (or binding) relationship. In truth they tear each other down. When it is all over, the only "winner" is the lawyer.

Swinging Bachelorhood

A survey of 2000 young men over eighteen, half of whom are single, revealed that "free-floating" sex is not all they thought it would be.[4] Over half of the men are not satisfied with their sex lives. The most surprising revelation to sex researchers is that most first sexual encounters are dismally disappointing due to absymal ignorance and unrealistic expectations. Unless treated by education or counseling, these sexual promiscuities can scar a marriage for life.

A few summers ago at our retreat on a lake in the northwoods of Wisconsin, I tuned into a radio station from the University of Wisconsin in Madison. Between musical programs, professors' and guest lecturers' speeches were presented. This particular evening the University chaplain spoke. I do not recall his exact words, but the gist of what he said was not preachy, but profound. He said in a memorable and intensely insightful short talk what everyone should hear about themselves. He talked about "sexual freedom" and its consequences on one's person.

In essence this is what he said: "Nothing is free. Someone, somewhere, sometime, pays for it. Giving a little bit of one's body here and there for one night or six months is not being fair to yourself. Because, along with giving up your body bit by bit, you give up bits and pieces of your psyche, your emotions, your will, your worth, your peace, your inner self. It takes a lifetime to become a whole person, an integrated person. Thus, while you are attempting to find yourself, to become a person you will like, you are breaking yourself up into little bits and scattering them here and there. Finally, you become so fragmented that, try as hard as did 'all the king's horses and all the king's men,' you will never be able to put yourself back together again. If you do find the one to whom you would like to commit yourself for a lifetime, you have but bits and pieces to offer. Think of that before you climb into bed with someone the next time."

Homosexuality

Another alternate lifestyle is homosexuality. Today it is considered a viable option with somewhat guarded acceptability by some "straights." Two men live together and engage in sexual practices. Sometimes they claim to fall in love and some go through ceremonies, not legally recognized, to become married to each other. On the surface, if one can accept the concept, it appears to be a good way out of marriage, family and responsibility.

It too, however, has drawbacks. Relationships become extremely complicated, and there is much floating in the homosexual community. It offers no "free ride." Witness the suit against tennis champion Billy Jean King for lifetime support by her lesbian lover.

Psychologists who work with homosexuals agree that when they become honest in their therapy sessions, ninety-nine percent are intensely unhappy. One of my friends who is a psychologist states that that figure is 100 percent. They are capable of terrible jealousy if their partner shows any sign of attraction to another person of the same or opposite sex. Homosexuals are subject to unusual and often fatal diseases because their bodies lose their immune systems. In fact, all of the free-floating sexual lifestyles can lead to devastating debilitation. Venereal diseases have become epidemic. One of these is called the new "sexual leprosy." Hot lines and VD clinics have sprung up across the country.

"Such is the predicament—indeed, the pathos—of herpes, one of the most common venereal diseases in the U.S. today, possibly even more widespread than gonorrhea. This year up to half a million more Americans will develop the telltale genital blisters of herpes, adding to the five million to fourteen million who already have the disease. When they seek medical help, they will often be given incorrect information or false hopes for cures. Most will suffer shame, guilt and even depression, and a few will become suicidal over what they feel is the 'new leprosy.' "[5]

Divorce

There is another option for the man who is married, the husband. He may decide not to be. He, or his wife, or both of them will decide to become ex-marrieds through divorce. New liberal laws make the divorce procedure simple, easy and short. Now it does not need to be contested. Some states call it dissolution. It has even become fashionable.

Six career women were interviewed on a television program. They were each asked about their marital status. Five were divorced, some more than once. One woman responded when she was asked about her status, "Of course I'm divorced. Who isn't? In the organization of which I am a part, you are not considered normal unless you are divorced."

There is no point to go into the details of the pros and cons of divorce. It is epidemic. It is hitting every kind of person, young, old, black, white, religious, non-religious, laborers, blue collar workers, executives, professionals in every field. It is a tragic mirror of the restlessness, rootlessness, self-indulgence and moral decay of our times. And there are no pat answers.

Husbands? They may choose not to be husbands. They have other choices: singleness, living together, bachelorhood, homosexuality or divorce. But this book is for and about those who do want to be married. Over seventy percent of both sexes do try marriage at some time in their life. Wives who want to keep the species—husband—alive and well must take their share of responsibility to make husband the most desirable and fulfilling of all the choices!

Chapter 9

Husbands: Sex—Strife and Serenity

By night on my bed I sought him whom my soul
loveth—
but I found him not.
How fair and pleasant art thou, O love, for delights!

The Song of Solomon

Not long ago Dear Abby ran a plaintive letter from a woman who called herself *Tired in Lincoln, Neb.* "At age 50, after 30 years of marriage, I would like to forget about sex altogether. Believe me, I've paid my dues. I suspect that many (if not most) women get very little physical satisfaction out of sex; they just go through the motions because they want to do something for the men they love. Please poll your readers, and if they're honest, I think you'll find I'm right."

In an article entitled "Refiguring a Sexual Equation," published in the *Los Angeles Times*, columnist Jim Sanderson reveals that:

To date, nearly a quarter of a million women have written in, and more than 50% agree with *Tired*. Absolutely astounding! Totally depressing. You thought it was the sexual revolution which was raising the divorce rate? It's the unsexual revolution. Can you imagine 30 years with a woman who was only "going through the motions"? How about 20 years? Ten years?

If *Tired* still loves her husband after 30 years he is not an animal; he is a human being who has responded to his wife's needs in many ways. You cannot believe the frustration (and ultimately the anger) a man feels in trying to excite and express his love to a woman who, month after month, year after year, is only "paying her dues". Quite often her passive resistance finally defeats him. He forgets the strength and joy he once knew. She emasculates him.

It's not just middle-aged women, either. The tragedy of our sexual revolution is both that it has overwhelmed some people and not touched others at all. Our society is interlaced with *Tired* females of all ages. Passive women who in a kind of smug, stubborn pride won't take charge even of their bodies, much less their lives. They won't make an effort to change, to grow. Their glory is to suffer nobly.

It's women who insist endlessly that they can't have sex without love. But how can a married woman have love without sex? Is it physically possible? Doesn't she see that sex is the very apex of love's pyramid—the final stage you move to when words and gestures do not suffice to express the depths of your feeling? Sex in marriage is love, the mystical union not only of two bodies but two souls. Marital love is debased when it really comes to mean nothing but affection, shared experience and kind words.[1]

It strikes me that a thoughtful wife will consider the possibility that to buy into *Tired's* concept of "paying her dues," may indeed contribute to further endangering husbands who are already an endangered species. As the columnist observed: "He (husband) accepts her view that sex is not very important. Maybe he lives out his life with her in that state—if some nubile young female doesn't come along to shock him into seeing what a shell of a male he's become."[2]

Henrietta welcomed us for breakfast in the sunny breakfast room of her beautiful mansion in the hills overlooking a great city. My husband and I were newly married. In addition, our simple, unsophisticated backgrounds betrayed us in such splendid surroundings.

Henrietta's husband had left early for work. As we sat down at her lovely table, she searched our faces for the self-conscious telltales of newlyweds. It was obvious she wanted to know what had happened in our bedroom the previous night. She made an oblique reference. We blushed, then, watched as her face grew stern. "We haven't done *that* for years." We were startled by her candor. Before we could respond in any way, she told us how unhappy and unsatisfying earlier efforts to have a sex life had been for her. She had been raised by strict parents who held somewhat less than healthy attitudes toward sex. These had been passed on to her. Her husband wanted sex she told us, but she knew it was wrong. Sex was only what a woman reluctantly tolerated to reproduce.

Henrietta was a beautiful woman, in her mid-forties, yet both she and her husband were suffering greatly because of jaded backgrounds, and lack of positive sex education. In a few months we heard about "another woman"; still later—divorce for Henrietta and her husband.

This story was repeated often a generation ago. But, is it repeated any less today? Sex education, of any type, was sparse then. Now there is information overload about everything, including sex! Are we any happier as a people and as a nation? Do we have longer marriages? Divorce thirty years ago was rare. Multiple divorce and remarriage was reserved primarily for Hollywood and high society. Rarely did "average" persons remarry after a divorce. Divorce simply would not happen more than once!

There has never been an era of "pure" morality. In the days of the Puritans, and later, Queen Victoria, right was right; wrong was wrong. But, no one would be foolish enough to believe that promiscuity, adultery and illegitimate pregnancies did not occur. However, the words "Victorian" and "Puritan" have become so distorted that most persons are ignorant about the history behind them. Perhaps the following brief, factual, historically authenticated statements will present a more balanced picture.

Contrary to what has been attributed to the reign of Queen Victoria—that it was one of sexual oppression and false modesty—she was a progressive monarch. She followed on the heels of the dissolute reign of George III whose rule was characterized by revolutions, war, class struggle and his eventual insanity.

Victoria fell in love and chose her husband, Albert. They had a happy marriage according to all history books. They had nine children. Hardly what one could call a prudish attitude about sex! Her reign saw more changes than any previous period in history. She revived faith in the crown. She captivated the affections of the multitudes and won the respect of thoughtful men. During Victoria's rule science, literature and the arts flourished. Medicine made great progress. Victoria herself was one of the first women to use an anesthetic in childbirth when she gave birth to Prince Leopold. This opened up a whole new attitude toward sex. Prior to that time, women avoided sex, partly because of the high mortality rate during birth by both mother and child.[3] Victoria mourned deeply for her husband, who died at the age of 41, and never remarried. One can not learn these things about a gracious monarch who made the crown a symbol of "private virtue and public honor" and ever again refer to "Victorian" as a "naughty" word.[4]

The same can be said about the Puritans. The glee with which "informed" teachers, professors and history writers fill the minds of vulnerable students about the "disgrace" of Puritanism reveals an absymal lack of information on their part, at best.

> Sarah Pierrepont and Jonathan Edwards, Puritan pastor-preacher, were married in 1727 after a courtship of four years . . . The Puritan view of marriage was not the restrictive and spiritless one usually assumed. Most Puritans had a healthy viewpoint toward marriage, sex and family life. Sarah in her wedding dress was "no white wraith mistily drifting toward some vague spiritual experience . . . but she wore a peagreen satin brocade with a bold pattern as she stepped joyfully toward her lover."
>
> Sarah and Jonathan were to have eleven children . . .

Every morning very early the family heard the father read a chapter from the Bible, and then ask God's blessing on the day ahead ... Each child had chores ... his tasks were chosen as largely as possible on the basis of special talents and wishes ...

Courtesy was the rule ... Edwards always gave one hour a day of complete attention to his children. Jonathan treated Sarah with total courtesy and serenely expected that each child would follow his example ... About four o'clock on fair afternoons, ... the couple would ride together in the hills above the river. Edwards would test the day's harvest of ideas against Sarah's practical intelligence.

In those Colonial days, most women lost their looks early. Not so, Sarah! Her husband appreciated her beauty and her style ... Though the Edwards had little money, Jonathan once spent eleven pounds for a gold chain and locket for his wife.

By 1900 (these) now maligned Puritans had produced: 13 college presidents, 65 professors, 100 lawyers, 30 judges, 56 physicians, 80 holders of public office, 3 U.S. senators, 3 mayors, 3 governors, a Vice-President of the United States, and a comptroller of the U.S. Treasury.[5]

If that is "Puritan," let's have more!

Fortunately there is a sense in which we have come full circle to the earthy awareness of Puritanism as it actually was. Sex has, thankfully, become an open subject. Extensive medical and psychological data has been gathered and well presented for the enrichment of the sexual relationship. The reader of such material can be the judge of what he or she can or cannot accept. My purpose, therefore, is not to add to the mass of data already available on sexual psychology and physiology. It is, rather, to present some basic common sense principles which have come through reading, discussions in groups and with individuals, and close up observations.

One of the most important lessons I learned was in a sociology course offered at one of our state colleges when I was a student. The registration in this course was always full because the subject of sex was to be covered. A generation ago, this was rare in any school at any level. Interest in the course, therefore, was high.

Out of an eighteen-week semester, to the disappointment of most, only two weeks were given to the subject of sexual physiology and sexual intercourse. We, as students, were not aware that the professor used a highly effective means of getting his point across. For sixteen weeks he talked about everything else in marriage but sex. The problems of money, in-laws, the likes and dislikes of married couples; how to adjust to each other; how to accept each other. He made it abundantly clear that the "chemistry" would wear off, and there were all kinds of adjustments to be made by both husband and wife throughout their marriage.

I shall never forget one glimpse he gave us of the way he and his wife worked at a particular irritation. "I am a bear in the morning when I awaken. But, my wife is usually bright. And, because we are two different people, whether body chemistry or whatever, we used to have horrendous fights in the morning. She couldn't understand why I was so grouchy. I could not understand her early morning buoyancy. It drove me wild! It took a long time for us to discover that her body chemistry was different from mine. So we made a rule that we would both remain silent until I had showered and dressed and had my first cup of coffee. That was the signal to talk to each other."

So simple a solution! (How many wars are waged between couples because of differing physical and psychological make-up.) Well, for weeks he discussed many problems which come up in a marriage. Through the years I have found his basic homespun wisdom to be of indispensable value. Finally, toward the end of the semester, he announced that the following Monday we would begin the discussion of sex. Monday morning came. Every student was there ahead of time!

The professor got up from his desk and moved to his lectern in the center of the lecture hall. "I am not surprised that Sociology 204 is one of the more popular classes on this campus. The subject matter we will now begin to deal with is the reason why you are taking this course. And I know what you are thinking: 'Right! It's about time you are finally getting to the good stuff.'" Loud laughter in the classroom.

"You have observed," he continued, "that for weeks we have dealt with the hard practical facts and problems which will sooner or later appear in all marriages. That's approximately 90% of the alloted semester time. I am sure you merely tolerated these sixteen weeks. Most of you paid very little attention to what went on because you were preoccupied with when I would get to this business of sex." Laughter again.

"That is the way it is with sex in marriage. Either it

will be a 10% factor, or an all-consuming 90% factor. If your marriage achieves the right kind of mutual satisfaction for both partners, it will be a 10% happy factor of your marriage. If a healthy sexual relationship is not achieved, it will be an all consuming 90% problem in your marriage! It will override any of the other problems."

That counsel was given by a sociology professor over thirty years ago and is still some of the wisest ever given. He knew that sex of itself is the barometer, not the thermometer, of a marriage. If things are right in the other areas of a marriage, sex usually will be fulfilling, and also "right."

The children in a nursery school class were making valentines for their parents. The teacher had written the words, "I Love You," for them to copy. One little boy worked very hard on his letters, painstakingly copying and erasing, then recopying. Finally, discouraged, he put his pencil down and sighed, "I just can't make love!" Often, that's the way it is in married life. But you see, one cannot make love on demand, physically or emotionally, any more than he or she can make peace, music, houses, bread, paintings or vaccines quickly. The word *make* derives from the Indo-European word *mag* which means to knead, to fashion, to fit. None of these processes are instant or immediate. They take time, and they require a learning process. And when learning evolves into the process of negotiating peace, the composing or performing of music, the building of houses, the making of bread, the painting of paintings, the formulating of a vaccine (from thousands of tests in a research laboratory), then finally process becomes art.

The "making" of love, emotionally, or physically, too, is an art. It is not what television, books, newsstand magazines and movies proliferate in billion-dollar industries. That is nothing other than the cheapest kind of hedonism—whether the jet set, movie stars, presidents, senators, ordinary citizens, or hookers are doing it!

Here are some practical suggestions which may help improve your sexual relationship with your spouse.

Sex is an art. It takes years of continuing learning on the part of both spouses. We are not born with all of the nuances of good sexual responses or initiations. They are learned. One of the most helpful things a husband and wife can do is take a long drive in the country rather than a short walk to the bedroom. During this extended drive talk out your feelings and inhibitions, what you like and don't like about the activities in your bedroom. Discuss how you can send "signals" to each other which are comfortable. Have a good "sex talk!" The cost of the gasoline on the road will be nothing compared with the rewards which will be reaped in the bedroom.

A sense of humor in sex can be a tremendous friend in growing together sexually. There will be trial and error, and need for much practice. If failures and blunders do happen, and they will, the ability to laugh will take away embarrassment and lay the foundation for sexual "success."

Sexual learning must never let up. This does not necessarily mean dozens of "positions." If a couple chooses only one "position" in a lifetime, there is yet a lifetime of sexual communication and communion to be learned. It's only when one or both of the partners thinks there is nothing more to try or learn that sex in marriage becomes perfunctory.

Intimacy. Intimacy is not merely the physical act of sex. Intimacy involves being together contentedly quiet. It is a pat on the shoulder, a kiss on the neck. A squeeze of the hand under the table, a gentle touching while driving the car.

Intimacy . . .

It is a thousand unspoken "I love you's" when husband or wife enters the room and eyes meet.

It is playing scrabble, roasting marshmallows, adding a note to Dad's (or Mom's) letter to the kids.

It is giving each other space and privacy when they need to be alone.

It is watching hubby ski after wife breaks her leg and can't ski with him.

It is spelling a word for him when he calls up and asks, "How do you spell . . . ?"

It is cooking chicken his favorite way when he has had a particularly rough day at work.

It is hubby taking coffee and toast to wife in bed.

Intimacy could be summed up for millions of wives

in this way: Learn to find the football and follow the quarterback. Bring on the popcorn and apples. Give your husband a rubdown during half-time on Monday night football!

Husbands need to be told they are accepted sexually by their wives. This is a sadly neglected area in many, if not most, marriages. One husband became vitally interested in the subjects I was writing about for this book. He was startlingly frank about his frustrations regarding sex in his marriage. "One of the biggest 'turn ons' to a husband is if a wife really enjoys sex and expresses that joy! I don't understand why, when women have become so aggressive in what they term 'a man's world,' they become suddenly so passive in the bedroom. Before all this push for 'rights' I could understand it. But now, why do they still play games when it comes to sex? I can provide for my wife, whom I love very much, what no one else can provide. I believe in 'till death do us part.' I intend to touch only this woman out of billions on this globe. But why doesn't she tell me when I please her? I don't know all there is to know about sex, but surely I must be doing *something* right. And what I'm not doing right I'm willing to learn. How I wish she would tell me when I cause her pleasure. I want her to anticipate our next sexual union as much as I do. In fact, I would be the happiest man on this planet if just once she would take the initiative and let me know she desires me! Please tell wives to verbalize to their husbands their sexual feelings. For many of us husbands, this never, or rarely, happens. We have no idea what our 'grade' is when we make love to them. Most of the time I do not know if I am passing or failing!"

From the *Los Angeles Times* article with which I began this chapter comes this helpful insight: "Most husbands are eager for their wives to have orgasms, the more the better, because this total physical abandonment emboldens and releases them, too. They are delighted with any kind of innovation or suggestion, no matter how self-centered, which indicates their wives are taking increased interest in sex. The power of male sex is highly dependent upon female desire."[6]

A common mistake (its universality is amazing) is that wives think their husbands can read their minds. They get into what I call a "scenario syndrome." They picture exactly how a particular evening might end, with candlelight, then touching, kissing, and the donning of a seductive nightgown. To their great dismay, then anger, the husband is not interested! It is as normal for husbands to not be interested at a given time as it is for wives. Allow for it. Let your husband in on the "scenario" you are setting up. He may or may not be in the mood for the idyllic scene. Perhaps the office or his job have gotten to him. Knowing your expectations will help him in any case.

Many times husbands ask, "Why didn't she tell me? I'm not a mind reader." Women's subtleties are not the same as those of men. Some tasteful directness must be involved. Wives must not go into a corner and lick their wounds when their husbands do not even know they have been wounded. Husbands do not mean to be insensitive. Every step sexually throughout a marriage must be learned. As I said in a previous chapter, just because a boy suddenly becomes a man, he does not necessarily know all about sex. Wives need to help their husbands learn together with them, to experiment and find new ways to enjoy each other's bodies.

"Throw away the book!" A gynecologist took keen interest in the unique emphasis of this book and generously gave of his time, commenting at length on some of the areas upon which I was writing. Among other things, he shared an incident involving one of his patients, anonymously, of course.

A woman in her thirties who had always been an "up" person came in to see him one day in a despairing state. She was alarmed at what was happening to her sexual relationship with her husband. He listened. She talked. She told him she had been meeting regularly for bridge and coffee at the home of some friends. A certain book was recommended by one of the women. She bought it, and started to read it. The more she read, the more depressed she became, and the more their sex life suffered. She "discovered" there was so much more to sex, and that she and her husband were obviously missing out on a great deal according to the book, and according to her friends.

"How was your sex life before you began to discuss it with these friends, and before you started to read the book?"

"It was terrific!"

"May I prescribe two things for you? One, throw

away the book. Two, change what you talk about at your kaffee-klatches, or change your friends!"

"She did both," the doctor grinned, "and she and her husband have a sexual relationship that suits them. After all—that's what matters, isn't it?"

"May I use that illustration?" I asked him.

Emphatically he gave assent. "I wish you would! And please add," he said as I walked out of his office, "those are two good prescriptions for all wives!"

Not quantity but quality. Sometimes sex will be highly passionate. Sometimes it will be quietly low-key. Sometimes it will be the highest expression of a couple's love for each other. At other times it will be contentedly "functional." Sometimes two bodies will be electrically alive, while at other times they receive each other calmly but give reassurance of deep inner love—a union of "knowing" each other. All of which means that healthy sex is not a matter of quantity, but quality.

Sex is celebration. "To celebrate something is to be in a joyful, thankful mood. The word 'celebration' has a festive, fun-filled air about it. And, at its best, sex in marriage is a celebration of joy.'"[7] Sex in marriage? What can it offer? Joy, pleasure, intimacy, contentment, satisfaction, giving, receiving, communication, communion, celebration, oneness, and wholesome sensuality. But not all of these expressions will be present in every sexual encounter! There may be none, there may be one, there may be several. It may go from sheer physical pleasure on one occasion to spiritual communion on another. Those who want the sex, but not the "building permit," think they can get "all of the above" instantly. Never! Whatever one calls the marriage contract—that "building permit," that "piece of paper"—the commitment, the entrusting, the bonding of one to the other for a lifetime will, in time, build "all of the above."

There is one more extremely important matter to discuss in this chapter. A young woman in her thirties sat in our living room, and finally, after much hedging, started hesitantly. "Last night when we were in bed, and getting ready to—well, you know—he couldn't do it! I just know he doesn't love me any more. I know there is someone else!"

I listened. Then I probed. Why did she think he did not love her? Why did she think there was "someone else?" Did she have any proof? What kind of day did he have? What has been happening at his work? What kind of pressure is he under? From everything I, as a lay person, could ascertain, this young man and his wife had experienced for the first time what is commonly called "impotency." What they, and many like them, did not know is that all men experience levels of potency. Such events as they had experienced are not cause to panic. Affirmation, empathy and gentle caring by a wife will help her man greatly.

> The responsiveness of both partners is based on their mutual acceptance as vulnerable human beings with unique needs, expectations and capabilities . . . Emotional needs, which vary with the mood, time and place, are not labeled "masculine" and "feminine" . . .
> Together they succeed or together they fail in the

sexual encounter, sharing the responsibility for failure, whether it is reflected in his performance or hers.

While conclusive proof is still lacking, there are firm grounds for believing that the female who esteems herself as something more than a collector's item—and who is responsive to her partner's needs as she wants him to be to hers—will do more to eliminate male fears of functional failure than all the therapy in the world.[8]

There is a bright side to the subject of sexual potency. For the first time medical science is suggesting that impotency, which was always pegged as psychogenic (emotional in origin), may be, in many cases, physiogenic (physical in origin). The February 15, 1980 issue of *Time Magazine* reported that out of 105 impotent males participating in a research project, thirty-five percent were of medical, not mental origin![9] The medical publication from which the report was taken indicated that once the defect was defined, appropriate therapy was instituted and, in many cases, potency was restored.[10] There is still much to be learned, but for men who have suffered the agony of lack of potency there is now medical hope.

Some years ago, when no older person dared to talk about such things, an eighty-year-old physician was invited to give a seminar to married couples about healthy sex in marriage. Few of us attending the seminar could understand why an eighty-year-old man should be conducting such a session. When he was introduced, we saw our answer. This man looked years younger than his octogenarian life span. He was charming, delightful and vigorous. He was still practicing medicine.

He set forth some of the most sensible principles for happy sex in marriage most of us had ever heard. Then he asked for questions. He winsomely put all of us at ease, which elicited frank questions from the group. One man felt so at ease he threw out the "pitch-of-the-season" question: "Doctor, how often do you and your wife have intercourse?"

The room was deathly silent, until the physician leaned against a table, crossed his arms and answered matter-of-factly, "Every night!" From out of the back row, a husband who obviously did not know he was expressing himself aloud, sighed for all to hear, "Wow!" The doctor thrust his head back and laughed hilariously.

He went on to explain that not every encounter ended in orgasm. "That isn't the real purpose of sex anyway," he added. "It has to do with communicating your feeling of oneness. Unfortunately," he concluded, "we've been taught to believe that at fifty, sixty, seventy or eighty—that's it. No more sex. My prescription is: Forget that nonsense and enjoy your God-given sexual capacities as long as you have life and health and strength!"

There are several billion people on planet earth. Out of that vast number there is only one person to whom you can give yourself entirely. One person whom you can "know" emotionally, intellectually, spiritually, mystically, and ever so intimately. And one person who can learn to "know" you in the same way. Such "knowing" is worth striving for.

The Gothic cathedrals that dominate the European landscape took centuries to build. A story is told of two masons who were helping to build one of these cathedrals. A passerby stopped and asked them, "What are you doing?" One answered, "I'm making bricks." The other replied thoughtfully, "I'm building a cathedral."

Those who opt for promiscuity, premarital sex, living together or "swinging," are making bricks. Those who work at healthy and complete sex in their marriage are building cathedrals.

Chapter 10

Husbands: Whole Is Better Than Perfect

That man is great, and he alone,
Who serves a greatness not his own . . .
Content to know and be unknown:
  Whole in himself.

Owen Meredith

A pastor preached to his small congregation about becoming perfect, as God is perfect. He explained that this is difficult, and to emphasize his point, he asked, "Does anyone know of a perfect person?" There was a pause. Then slowly, waveringly, a hand went up in the back row. The pastor was surprised. He asked the question again to make sure he had not been misunderstood. Again the hand went up. "Sir," questioned the pastor, "do you really know someone who is perfect?" "Yes, sir," the voice was timid, but the answer decisive, "my wife's first husband!"

Sally, a young bride, stopped by to see me one afternoon. She and Tom had been married for nearly a year. She had obviously come to talk about their marriage. I asked how things were going between them. "Okay, I guess," she answered reflectively. "But Tom —really—well—I wish that when he comes home from work he would help me get dinner and pick up things. He leaves his stuff all over the house. I have to pick up his trousers and hang them up, and put his dirty socks in the laundry. I wish he were more like Ted. He helps Sue in the kitchen, and he even folds the laundry. Tom is a good husband, but I think Ted is just about perfect."

I thought, "Perfect, huh?" I proposed that in time she could gently lead Tom into helping a bit around the house, perhaps by making an appointment for a work time and by having a list ready for him. I did wonder about Ted, however. Within a few weeks I found out. Sue stopped by to help me with a project. We outlined some ideas, and stopped for a cup of coffee. "How's Ted? I haven't seen him for a while to 'howdy' with him. I know you two are really crazy about each other."

Sue set her cup down, paused, then opened up. "I really am glad you asked. I was afraid to bring it up, but I have to talk to someone." My heart sank. Was this another marriage going down the tubes?

She continued, "Ted is really a dear husband. But he drives me nuts! He's—what do you call it—hyperthyroid? He won't sit down for a minute when he gets home from work. I was so happy to discover before we were married that he could cook, though I'm not too bad at it. But he comes into the kitchen, tastes the soup or gravy, or salad dressing and tells me what to add. He won't let me buy the 'bought' kind. He hates it. He picks up everything as soon as I lay it down, washes it, puts it away just when I need to use it again. He washed the eggbeater four times the other evening. And, he's the only man in the whole world who comes home and cleans out things every night— kitchen cupboards, dresser drawers. He does the laundry. He can't stand crumbs in the silverware tray. Our garage is so clean we could eat off the floor. I wish he were more like Tom—easy going—and wouldn't come apart when I don't put the cap on the toothpaste. Tom must be a perfect husband."

Perfect . . . That word again! If *perfect* is equated with "the way I want you to be," it should be eliminated from the vocabulary. Each of these wives, though she loved her own imperfect husband dearly, was absolutely sure the other wife had everything in her perfect spouse. And this perception is not at all uncommon. Rarely is it the husband a wife *has*, who has all the good qualities. Usually, it's some other gal's guy.

"Why don't you fix things like George does?"

"Do you always have to eat so fast?"

"Couldn't you at least set the table like Jane's husband?"

"When we courted, you always put your arm around me in the car."

"I know why you want to kiss me. Just so you can have sex."

"You don't love me. You'd rather go bowling every Thursday night."

"Why do you wake up slowly in the morning?"

"Why do you jump up right away in the morning? Why don't you hold me?"
"Why don't you mow the lawn? Pete is always
working in the yard."
"Why *did* you mow the lawn? You cut down all
my tulips."

One husband said, "A lot of women think that getting a husband is like buying a used car. You don't
see it like it is, but like it's going to be when you get it
fixed up."

Husbands, too, look for the perfect spouse and can
be just as picky. But, for now, let's set aside the husbands' hang-ups and concentrate on helping this endangered species.

Though there is increasing effort being made to prepare young couples for some of the realities of marriage, it is not nearly enough. Pastors across the
country are toughening the rules for couples who
want to get married. Some couples must take special
courses and temperament analysis tests. Many pastors refuse to marry couples who are not teachable
and whose immaturity is obvious. The State of California requires very young couples to undergo several
sessions of counseling to try to prepare them for marriage and, often, immediate parenthood. This is all
encouraging, but it is a drop in the bucket.

What is "perfect marriage"? It is not, as one cynic
described, "a marriage in which the husband snores
and the wife is deaf." In the sense that the person a
woman marries will be the answer to every one of her
problems, bring everlasting happiness, and fulfill all

her expectations—in that sense—it is unattainable and unrealistic. It is a marriage in trouble before "I do" is uttered.

Yet, countless couples who see around them half of their friends' marriages falling apart—and who know that there will be struggle in their own marriage—still look to their partner to make theirs that "perfect marriage." They exempt themselves from responsibility. And the disappointed Sallys and Toms, and Sues and Teds, continue to believe that if each of their partners were different they would have a "perfect marriage."

The single most important and fundamental thing married couples ought to know, but are not taught is: They married each other to be together on the same team!—to root for "the team" on the same side, not the opposite side, of the stadium! Even when a couple is in disagreement, they are not enemies! They are teammates! They become members of the "Let's-face-life-together" team. And they share mutual responsibility for making their team a winner.

Everything worthwhile in life involves struggle. Why, then, are newly marrieds, from totally different backgrounds, surprised when they begin to struggle in the area of learning how to live together? Each may have come from a good family and parents who had a good marriage. Yet, more than likely, he or she had hassles with brothers and sisters. And, if they probe just a bit they'll discover their parents had differences. Why, then, such surprise when their first disagreement occurs?

The romance, the courtship, the sexual intimacy during the honeymoon are all beautiful, wonderful, early stages of the "mating dance" and celebration. They are the beginnings of a relationship which will go through many phases and transitions and painful processes, all of which can bring two people together or tear them apart, depending on the couple's willingness (or lack of it) to grow.

A speaker addressed a group of young people: "Oh, how very much in love my wife and I were when we were first married. We thought we could not possibly be more in love—ever! Now, thirty-three years and thousands of struggles later, that attraction seems like a summer camp romance." Their eyes, faces and body language evidenced that kind of mature love. What a pity if they had stayed back there in the "romance-on-cloud-nine" phase!

Wouldn't it be sad if two people—a husband and wife—after maturing physically for thirty-three years, were "in love" in exactly the same way as they were on their wedding day? It would be much like a lovely little brand new, just born baby! What a marvelous manifestation of God's creative work! "The baby is perfect!" says the doctor who holds it up for the mother to see.

"What a perfect baby!" marvels the mother as she holds it for the first time.

"What a perfect son! He kinda, sorta, looks like me!" brags the human co-creator to his wife.

"The most beautiful perfect baby I have ever seen!" exclaim the doting grandparents. And that tiny baby's perfection is a miracle in which everyone takes delight. Days, weeks and months pass. Is that little, tiny baby still as little, tiny and "perfect" as the day on which it was born? Everyone who took such joy in that "perfect" little baby would experience great grief if it stayed exactly like it was the day it was born—if it did not go through the normal struggling processes of growing and maturing out of one phase into the next.

A tiny baby is supposed to grow. It must learn to roll over by itself. It must notice its hands. It must become aware of life around it. It should smile and laugh out loud. Then get up on all fours. Crawl, stand, and prepare for that marvelous First Step! The folks around it—parents, grandparents, older brothers and sisters—join in helping the baby progress to that moment when it's able to stand on its own two feet! They delight in the growth and development of that "perfect" baby.

In a few years the baby becomes Junior or Juniorette —no longer a baby! Now begins another process, often painful, of guiding the child into a new phase of the growth process: becoming independent of its parents. By means of a thousand processes thereafter, and throughout the rest of that child's life, he or she will have to learn in a multitude of ways the myriad of things there are to learn. Even as that child learns to become a whole person, so, too, a healthy marriage is a learning process. Relationships, like the people who share them, do not arrive fully grown. They must be worked with and worked on as they proceed through various stages to maturity.

Another important thing for a couple to be aware of is the influence of "role transference." My father was "up with the birds and in bed with the chickens" every day of his life. At first he was a farmer, then a mechanic, and then part owner of a small business. His was a twelve-hour day, with little time for relaxation and fun. Later, with the remaining family, he moved to another city where he got an eight-to-five job in a factory. Thus I was thoroughly conditioned to think: a husband-father gets up at dawn and engages in physical work, comes home at 5:20 and has dinner exactly at 6:00. If he doesn't, he isn't working. My father did most of the outside work, and mother did the inside work. He fixed things, built fences, painted the house, and sanded the hardwood floors. I knew he worked because I saw the end product he produced.

When my husband and I were married, the "role transference" from my father and the concept of what work was all about was a serious problem for me. My husband was preparing for a nurturing, caring profession, which embraced the world of ideas. He dealt with abstract rather than material, tangible, end products. His work hours required most of each day and nearly every night. A few mornings a week he had to sleep and relax, to make up for counseling, meetings, and conferences, some of which went beyond midnight. When he came home, physically he was there. Mentally, he was working. He produced no visible product in his dealings with committees, individuals, people with problems, and "problem people." Dinner in our home for all of our years together is to this day anywhere between 6:00 and 10:00 P.M.

I did not realize for years the tremendous stress factor in his work until, in desperation, I sought counsel. The counselor informed me that the physical work I had seen my father do was quite unlike the stress-producing factors in my husband's job. The creative "brain-drain" and emotional demands of his profession are for specially equipped persons. But equipped as he was, it would take its toll on him, and our marriage. How far was *I* willing to go? My "role transference" from my father to my husband had to stop. My husband had to be freed to do what his "inner calling" called him to do, or he would never achieve his whole personhood. A wise young minister, with whom I am acquainted, counsels young men and women about marriage. He advises, "We all need to be 'saved' from our parental families when we establish our own." He is saying in his way what the Creator said, ". . . a man shall leave his father and mother and be united to his wife."[1]

I confess that it hasn't been easy dealing with the unrealistic expectations of having a perfect "romance-on-cloud-nine" marriage. What I'm learning, however, is that since there is no perfect person, man nor woman; one cannot expect perfection to come out of imperfection. If the expectation that it could were set down as a mathematical equation, it would read:

One Imperfect Person + One Imperfect Person =
One Perfect Marriage

The French have a word which applies here. It's the same in English: impossible!

One woman, with whom I had occasion to visit with briefly in a supermarket, told about the impending marriage of one of her children. She hoped the marriage would last, as do all parents these days. "I have come to the conclusion that marriage boils down to adjusting to each other's idiosyncrasies," she stated. There is truth in what she said. But, the more I contemplate it, the more I wonder if that is what God wants in a healthy marriage. I keep coming back to the principle that the goal in growing is wholeness, not just adjusting.

A few years back a politician coined a word which became foreign policy: *accommodation*. Today we see the results of accommodation to the idiosyncrasies of hundreds of nations who have taken full advantage of our sometimes one-sided accommodation to them. To merely accommodate or adjust to our marriage partner is a distortion of the harmony which results when we become whole persons. Accommodation can result in a loss of personal identity or relational vitality. When my husband and I reach this state of accommodation—"Okay, I will put up with him (or her)," before long we've stalemated, stagnated, stopped growing. We may want adjustment, but we need creative partnership. Which is to say: "Whole is better than perfect." Each partner must become whole!

My young friend, Todd, stopped by our house. I asked him what he thought about marriage. Todd is only twenty, but he gave a profound answer: "Unless I am ready *not* to be married, I am not ready to *be* married. If I marry because I am unhappy, insecure, or have a need, and blindly decide that getting married is the answer to all of these needs and expectations, I am a very foolish man. When I find that right woman, I want us both to be whole. Because if one or the other leans too hard on the partner, we'll both go down."

Todd's wisdom awed me: Wholeness equals two persons standing alone before they can stand together.

UCLA psychiatrist Dr. Roger Gould believes that two people marry each other to achieve qualities in the other partner which they feel they lack. Gradually they begin to claim these qualities unknowingly and possessively, and this leads to problems. It is imperative that each spouse complete his or her own growth process, or there will be marital disaster. "The growth process is relentless." he states.[2]

The growth process is the "becoming-whole" process. They cannot be separated. Dr. Gould says, in essence, that we try to complete ourselves by marrying someone else. Some years ago, this was an acceptable way to look at the marriage union. Two people were halves, and in marriage they became whole. It seemed a good idea in more innocent times. But, media information, advanced education for the masses, the feminist movement and, especially, new understanding about self-identity and becoming whole, obviates much of that view of marriage.

The concept of learning wholeness is gaining popularity. In some instances it involves moving into an isolated atmosphere for many weeks where a rigid regimen is followed. Special healthful diet, physical exercise, and meditative introspection are involved. The emphasis is holistic not perfectionistic.

This is not new. When Jesus of Nazareth said two millenia ago, "Be perfect," He meant, "Become whole."[3]

Marriage is never static. About the time marriage partners think they have it all together, another phase of life begins and they must both go to work on it. This is not a minus. It is a plus. If we learn to see the growing pains in marriage as being positive, the relationship will never lose its challenge or excitement. It is only when the partners stop growing in wholeness together that life and marriage lose meaning. Rodney Dangerfield, the comedian, has a routine in which he says, "My wife and I sleep in separate rooms. We have dinner apart. We take separate vacations. We are doing everything to keep our marriage together." Well, it need not be that way if we know and live by the principle that whole is better than perfect.

How then do we go about growing, becoming whole, becoming perfect, in the sense of becoming complete? In one of the first sharing groups with which I became involved, I found an important clue. We were reading and reacting to the profoundly simple insights of an English Quaker lady set forth in a book published over a hundred years ago. It could have been written today. Hannah Whitall Smith's *The Christian's Secret of a Happy Life*[4] never ceases to astound me. Every time I peruse its pages I am enriched. She covers every base in practical earthly living, and in heavenly spiritual living.

On this matter of growing and becoming whole, she makes such marvelous sense. The truth she articulates has been there all the time, but so few of us have seen it. She explains the concept of an inner life principle which cannot help but grow. Plant an apple seed and grow an apple. Plant a flower seed and get a flower. The salmon "plants" a salmon egg and pro- duces a baby salmon. The wind scatters dandelion seeds and up come dandelions. The father fertilizes the mother's seed and a baby begins to grow. Each of these marvelous creative seeds will grow and produce "after its kind" when placed in an atmosphere which is conducive to growth.

The apple seed needs fertile ground; the flower needs nourishment; the salmon needs cold, fresh water; the baby needs a womb. And, believe it or not, they just grow. The apple seed does not strain and flagellate itself insisting, "I must grow into an apple." The salmon egg does not cry out to the thousands of other eggs, "I want to be a salmon, not a frog!" The baby seed does not fret about becoming a human be- ing. It is destined to be that by virtue of a remarkable "inner life principle."

"See how the lilies of the field grow. They do not labor or spin."⁵ They just grow and become beautiful lilies. How different from our bootstrap human striv- ing to be dressed like "Solomon in all his splendor."⁶ What release would come to many . . . what freedom from relentless striving toward growth or becoming whole, if they got hold of the liberating truth that the loving Father has given them lots of room in which to grow.

This was articulated by King David when he reflect- ed on how God had worked with his spinning, toil- ing, sometimes recalcitrant children to bring them into a large, broad place of their own. "He brought me out into a spacious place; he rescued me because he de- lighted in me."⁷ He delighted in me? Why would he delight in me? Because He made me, loves me, sent His Son to redeem me and to place within me that "inner life principle" which says you shall not remain where you now are. You shall become all you're meant to be.[8] I have given you loads of space in which to grow and experience what life in Me is all about. And the closer you get to Me the more room there is!

Our daughter, Julie, got so excited about this concept set forth in one of David's songs that she composed a song of her own. The loving Father is speaking and He says:

> Come on into My room, it's the best place to be.
> It's a room with a view and the rent is free.
> So kick your shoes off and feel right at home,
> 'Cause you'll find there's space at My place
> Where there's room to grow.

The exciting truth that the Father longs for His children to become complete and whole was reinforced by my best Friend, often referred to as the Great Physician. On one occasion He said to a troubled man, "Do you want to be whole?" When you read the report of what happened next, you discover, amazingly, that this troubled man was not all that sure. He had been an invalid for thirty-eight years and appeared to have adapted to his crippled state. Perhaps that's why Jesus singled him out and asked, "Do you really want to get well?" The man equivocated, "No one will help me. Everyone gets in line ahead of me. They make it impossible for me to get there from here!"[9]

Perhaps it was with righteous irritation—"white anger"—that, without giving him a helping hand, Jesus commanded, "Get up! And don't leave your bed there, take it with you!" Faced with his moment of truth, the troubled man made a decision. He got up! And he picked up his bed roll too! He was healed physically and in the process the Scripture suggests he was also made whole mentally, attitudinally, emotionally.

It may or may not be a physical handicap which precipitates an encounter with Jesus, but for everyone there comes a moment of truth when he or she is confronted with the need to make a personal, conscious, deliberate decision and connect up with Jesus who said, "I have come that they may have life, and have it to the full."[10]

One evening an elitist religious leader approached the Nazarene with a question about this matter of being whole. "Flesh gives birth to flesh,"[11] Jesus explained. Each of us was born physically and, because it is a natural law of living things, each of us will grow physically without working at it. Then He added, "The Spirit gives birth to spirit."[12] With those words Jesus opened up a whole new realm of growth and attainment and explained that this happens as a result of spiritual birth, variously called: conversion, being born again, entering into a personal relationship with Jesus. "You must be born again,"[13] He said. When that happens—through the power of an inner life principle which cannot help but grow—completeness will come. Naturally, spontaneously and joyfully you will move toward maturity in God's big, wide, wonderful and spacious place.

The growing process includes the principle that everyone has "ingredients" within him or her which, when discovered and developed and utilized, will help him or her become a complete, interesting and terrific person. Everyone has certain obvious natural talents—musical, artistic, mechanical, mathematical, physical, etc. Everyone also has special talents or gifts unthought of as such. They are character traits which positively motivate that person to do what he or she does. I call them "what-makes-you-tick" gifts. (At this point, for the sake of clarity and brevity, the pronoun "he" will be used. I will address myself to gifts and their application as they apply to husbands, although, as I've said, both male and female have them.)[14]

1. One of these is the gift of *convincing*. The husband with this gift is sold on what he believes and wants others to be as sold as he is. There are no grays to him and a woman married to a spouse with this gift may feel dominated by her husband. This need not be the case. Convincers are reasonable people, they simply need to be heard. Then they are usually ready for others to present their views. A wise wife will provide the opportunity for conviction to be presented clearly and without argument. This is a wonderful gift. A convincer, if encouraged, can be a responsible husband and leader.

2. Another gift is that of *serving*. Few persons want to serve or be servants in our self-centered society. However, I know a corporate executive with this gift. He jumps up to greet a guest in the home or in the office. He remembers if his guests like coffee black or with cream. He helps serve dinner, or will cook it to

surprise his wife. He anticipates a need and acts upon it, before it is expressed. A person with the gift of serving may find himself busy from early morning until late at night because he finds it difficult to say no to others. This may make his wife unhappy at times. But an appreciative wife will gently suggest how he can let others "have a piece of the action" so neither she nor he is overwhelmed by his desire to serve. A wise wife whose husband has this gift will realize she has a rare, beautiful diamond for a husband.

3. Another "what-makes-you-tick" gift is that of *learning*. The person who has it may gain a Nobel prize for research. But not usually. The most improbable person may have this gift. He may want to learn all there is to know about electronics, flying, bread-making, orchid-raising, macrame, photography, wildlife or covered bridges. The learner-student may not ever venture into applying what he learns in a practical way. He just enjoys learning about everything. He may spend hours alone and not have any awareness of time. He may forget dinner and be up into the wee hours. A wife should not come apart at this seeming inconsideration. A husband with this gift, in a day when many minds atrophy from lack of use, can make a marriage excitingly interesting. The wise wife of a husband with this gift will enter into his world with encouragement and enthusiasm rather than complain. Not only will she learn information about his world, she will learn about the inner spirit and soul of her husband, that will bring them both into true intimacy so desperately needed in a good marriage.

4. A fourth such motivational gift is that of *problem-solving*. This person is not a theoretician. He is highly practical. He is a tackler of problems. He delights in personal and group encounters which result in new insights for himself and others. He likes enthusiastic people who respond to him, and who are eager to follow specific steps of action. He perceives life's situations and experiences and wants to help if help is needed. He does not—like the theoretician or learner —gather information for the sake of information and knowledge. He may seem to oversimplify life with his action-answers, but a keen gift of perception usually accompanies problem-solving. He does not go off the deep end, but he seeks validity and knowledge to help solve practical or "people" problems. The person with this gift may appear to take over every situation. But, he does not do so because he wants to dominate. This gift is a forceful one. One who has it cannot stand to see problems left unsolved, whether it's a leaky roof, or a person who needs help with a serious problem. An unwise wife will complain about others' demands on her spouse. A wise wife will see this as a gift which gives a sense of purpose to her husband. Another bonus is that he will drop everything to help her when she has a problem. What a gift!

5. Can you believe that another gift that turns some people on is *giving*? Forty years ago Lloyd Douglas wrote a book entitled *The Magnificent Obsession*. It is the story of a rich man who dedicated his latter years to giving away fortunes to deserving persons—anonymously. It may be a matter of interest that many people with the gift of giving are not rich, however,

but the person with this "what-makes-you tick" gift is unselfish and other-person oriented. How much he has is simply not a factor. He sees a material need and takes care of it. He is not mesmerized by the "when my ship comes in, I will give generously" cliche. If a husband has the gift of giving, a wise wife will not attempt to squelch it. First, because to do so will take away his joy. Secondly, because his wife will be the greatest recipient of this gift. While he will never be a spendthrift—that's why he is able to give—he will make her happy with unexpected little gifts when it is not her birthday or Christmas. Better yet, he will not only give things, he will give of himself. What more can a wife want from her husband?

6. Another "what-makes-you-tick" gift is that of *organization*. Without this gift, every institution in society would collapse, including marriage. A physician and his wife were heading for serious trouble in their marriage. The problem was extremely simple, but because of society's view of "husbands' work" and "wives' work" they tussled for years over paying the household bills. He always paid them late. They both had been taught that a man is not a man, nor is he head of the house, if he doesn't take care of the bank account. This doctor loved to work in his greenhouse and putter in the kitchen—"woman's work." His wife had a flare for "getting things done." She could organize almost anybody to accomplish anything. She loved accounting. This doctor and his wife were invited to a sharing group where they discovered gifts that are neither masculine nor feminine. They also identified their gifts and began learning how to enjoy

and affirm each other in the exercise of these gifts. Today their marriage is on sound footing. He putters in the greenhouse and the kitchen—a therapeutic diversion from his profession. She manages the household, pays the bills, oversees their financial investments, and plans vacations. And they both love every minute of it.

7. The physician noted above had the next "what-makes-you-tick" gift, that of *compassion*. This compelling concern focused on a sick plant in his greenhouse as well as the patients in his clinic. A compassionate man may seem feminine because he is gentle, caring, often soft-spoken. He may not rough-and-tumble with his children because that's not his thing. But he senses hurt and distress and tries to help lessen both. He also can sense phoniness and insincerity ten miles away because he is so finely tuned to the deep needs and hurts of others. His wife and others may misread this gift and charge him with being guided by emotions rather than logic. He may seem devoid of convictions, but convictions lie deep within him and will surface when the demand arises. A wife married to a man gifted with compassion at first may feel he is not strong or directive. That he is not a leader. But "still water runs deep" applies to such a husband. And that fortunate wife has the best of both worlds.

There are loads of other gifts in addition to various combinations of the above. The gifts of laughter, tears, enthusiasm, firmness, perseverance, anger (used wisely), reflectiveness and faith, all contribute to making a man interesting, exciting, enchanting. Helping her husband discover, develop and exercise these gifts may provide his wife with her greatest reward.

A famous, highly gifted individual, with a glittering array of talents and abilities, commented, "I am so tired of people praising me for what I do. I wish sometime someone would praise me for who I am. I feel so person-less!" Can you imagine what would happen if, instead of criticizing what a husband does, his wife would praise him for who he is? Truly, she could help him become whole, which is better than perfect, and in the process move toward further wholeness for herself.

Chapter 11

Husbands:
How to Preserve the
Species

To strive, to seek, to find, and not to yield.
Alfred Tennyson

There is a fable about a contest between North
Wind and the Sun. North Wind bragged he would
force the mantle off an old man walking alone down a
country road. Sun deferred to North Wind to try his
way first.

North Wind began to blow chilling breezes. The
man quickened his pace. North Wind blew stronger
and more furiously and sent icy blasts upon the old
man. The more North Wind blew and chilled, the
more tightly the old man pulled his coat about him,
and pressed his face down into a well-worn muffler.
Finally, North Wind gave up and stilled the storm.

Sun came out from behind the clouds and beamed
bright rays which warmed the air about the old man.
His grip on his coat loosened. His face came up out of

the muffler. Sun's warming rays continued to beat down upon a radiant countryside. The man slowed his walk, smiled, looked about him, up to the blue sky, and at the silver sunlight dancing on bright red maple leaves.

Sun continued to shine long warming rays upon the old man and the beautiful scene around him. Slowly the man unwound the muffler from his neck, took off his mantle and slung it over his arm. Briskly he headed up the hill, whistling a tune to let his wife know he would soon be home.

Hopefully, as a result of reading this book, other wives will come to understand, as I have, the tremendous influence we have in the lives of our husbands. It is an influence which we, as wives, can exercise in constructive or destructive ways. We can, like North Wind, try to exert our power in a manner which has chilling consequences. Or, we can beam bright warmth in a way which makes a positive contribution toward helping preserve the endangered species— *husband*.

When I started to write this book I believed the title would provoke thought. I felt the parallelism of endangered wildlife and the human species—husband— was striking. Purporting a thesis is easy. Supporting that thesis is not easy. In fact, it required long hours of research and writing. I knew when I began that the premise was sound. I know now I had underestimated its profundity.

The Endangered Species Act enacted by Congress in 1966 for the preservation of wildlife sets forth a program "for the conservation, protection, restoration

and propagation of selected (endangered) species."
Everything in this book is an attempt to conserve,
protect, restore and propagate the species *husband*,
and to preserve the awesome wonder and beauty of
the living organism—marriage. Though practical
suggestions have been given throughout the book, I
would like to zero in on something specific about
"conserve, protect, restore and propagate.

To conserve: In modern game preserves, animals are
given the best of care, love, balanced diet, protection
from the elements, and a balanced planned ecosystem. No person can have a totally controlled environment, but as wives we can contribute much to make
our husband's environment as peaceful, healthful and
creative as possible. We can balance the ecosystem
into which husband returns each evening—a friendly
"Hi, honey, how was your day?" even if yours was
bad; a picked-up house; minimal confusion by children and family and pets. We can give some expression of love. (How often we wives have the martyred
hangdog look from a leftover "mad" when husband
went to work early in the morning!) No one likes to be
ignored and we wives have a special proclivity for ig-
noring husbands when we want to punish them—including withholding sex. Husbands generally are
overt. Wives often are covert. We play our games, but
they serve to destroy a relationship, and they further
endanger our chances to keep, conserve, our husbands.

We can also provide a balanced diet and encourage
exercise. Many animals get fed better than do husbands. Some wives may think that a "good meal"

consists of mashed potatoes, gravy, biscuits, steak and pie. Not so. We must learn about and implement good nutrition. Heavy meals and junk foods around the house will do much to further endanger the species. Nagging won't get husband to exercise. Wife's setting the example may. Exercise can become a beautiful togetherness.

To protect: We can provide a haven for our husbands when they return home. They are out in a fiercely competitive world. They deserve to find refuge in a friendly cooperative houshold. Instead of scheduling repairs and chores on evenings and weekends, schedule a regular time for fun with each other with the television turned off. If we wives would plan creative fun times and special events, perhaps our husbands' dazed television stares would become seeing, loving times to share.

To restore: The women's movement, for better or for worse, has confused, frustrated, concerned and, in some instances, angered our men. A wife is the only person who can restore to her husband a renewed sense of worth, respect, dignity and honor. She must never "put him down" regardless of who's at fault (and the fault may be his in a given situation). We wives must restore to our husbands faith in their maleness, their specialness and their right to be human!

To propagate: Perhaps the most effective thing you can do for your husband is to allow yourself to be imperfect. You may begin to love yourself for the first time in your life. By allowing yourself imperfection, you will find it easier to love and accept him as he

is—another imperfect creature of God like you. You
will propagate (transmit) to your offspring and others
an example of what a healthy husband-wife relationship can be. This kind of propagation will do much to
preserve your husband, and others, by your wise example.

"When you love someone you do not love them all
the time, in exactly the same way, from moment to
moment. It is an impossibility. It is even a lie to pretend to and yet this is exactly what most of us demand. We have so little faith in the ebb and flow of
life, of love, of relationships. We leap at the flow of
the time and resist in terror its ebb. We are afraid it
will never return. We insist on permanency, on dura-
tion, on continuity; when the only continuity possible, in life as in love, is in growth, in fluidity—in
freedom, in the sense that dancers are free, barely
touching as they pass, but partners in the same pattern. The only real security is not owning or possess-
ing, not in demanding or expecting, not in hoping,
even."[1] We do not own our husbands. They are
loaned to us for a lifetime. We can give them the gift
of longer life and ourselves the treasure of compan-
ionship in our sunset years.

There are many words in our language today which
are strictly "dictionary" words because we have heard
them so often they have no meaning. Words like love,
commitment, communication, sacrifice, unselfish-
ness, loyalty, and others. Here are six different
expressions of those same words—each beginning
with the letter H—to serve as mental pegs on which to
hang some thoughts on how we can help preserve

our men, our husbands. Have. Hold. Help. Harbor. Hear. Handle.

1. HAVE: Commitment

An elderly couple was interviewed on television. Because they had been married for forty-five years, they were supposed to be authorities in the field of marriage. Said the wife, "We're not experts—we're students!"

One of my favorite actresses appeared on a talk show—mind you, nothing religious—but a woman with a decent view of husband-wife relationships. In response to the host, who intimated that her marriage of many years was a rarity in her business, she said, "Yes, but anyone can spread herself thin. A real woman makes one man feel privileged!"

"To have and to hold." An archaic expression of an old-fashioned marriage ceremony? Not to those who translate it into contemporary terminology: guarantee, promise, secure, contract, affirm, bind, risk!

When the nation of ancient Israel walked across a dried up river bed to gain her promised land, she experienced risk. Soon the Jordan would return to flood tide, cutting off any possibility of retreat.[2] She was committed "to strive, to seek, to find, and not to yield."[3] No matter how formidable her task there was no turning back. But she could not "have" her promised land unless she was prepared to give her full commitment.

"To have" is a verb, not a noun. It implies continuing action. Some months ago I baited a young woman. "Jill, I asked, "how long is a marriage vow supposed to last?" She had just told me of the heart-breaking divorces of several of her best friends. She looked at me in utter disbelief. "Until one of the part-ners dies, isn't that it? That's my intention. But then, look what happened to two of my closest friends."

What has happened to commitment? It seems that today vows are not taken seriously. If it doesn't work, we retreat, withdraw, punish, put up with, exist . . . divorce. Do we wish to make a positive contribution to the preservation of the man we married, or will marry? We can start by accepting the premise that the commitment in marriage, "to have", is commitment beyond any possibility of retreat. It is made of steel, not straw.

There is another facet to commitment which is al-most completely overlooked in today's self-gratifica-tion climate. This commitment, if applied when all else fails, may keep the marriage intact.

Every couple knows there are times when the mar-riage is so stressed and strained that the concept of commitment to the *spouse* is virtually impossible. As with the pupal stage of the butterfly, the marriage hangs by a thread.

At this crucial stage, when it seems impossible to commit themselves to each other for a period of time, the partners' commitment to *marriage* itself, and to their *vows* before God, can and will take over.

Like the chrysalis, if couples hang on, they will emerge in a more mature "stage" *because they commit-ted themselves to the commitment.*

This commitment to the ultimate commitment of a God-ordained marriage is the steel out of which real marriage is forged.

2. HOLD: Support

The hold of a ship is a fascinating place. I have seen the row beams, the supports, the dark nooks and caverns for the storage of cargo on great ships on which I have traveled, such as the Queen Elizabeth and Queen Mary. But I was surprised and aghast at the water seepage into the hold, some of which became murky, poisonous bilge. Shipbuilders and designers are well aware of this, and outfit these great ocean liners with an efficient pumping system to eradicate excess water and bilge. It is interesting to me that though passengers on a luxury liner in fancy suites and staterooms may know there is constant, continual murky bilge seeping into the hold, they do not abandon ship.

Marriage, too, like a ship, has its constant seepage and bilge. It is an integral part of a binding lifelong relationship. But there must be a cleansing "pumping out"—not a "bailing out" as many want to do—of this potentially poisonous seepage. Let us be to our husbands that hold, that support, which encourages him to establish a healthy pumping system for marriage bilge. The weather may get stormy. At times we will get seasick. But we mustn't bail out and abandon ship. There are marvelous by products to such "holding."

"To hold" means we support our husbands. The kind of support I refer to is that which holds up husbands in their "up-ness" and "down-ness"—support which makes us interested in their activities; which encourages them to find out what their talents and gifts are, and supports them in fulfilling those inner creative needs and desires. "To hold" our men is to free them to initiate the act of becoming by letting them know we love and accept them as they are. It may sound scary, or even weird, to suggest that to free is to hold. However, the wisest One who ever lived said exactly that: "If you cling to your life, you will lose it; but if you give it up for me, you will save it", adding, on another occasion, "When you did it to these my brothers you were doing it to me!"[4] When we give our husbands up to the freedom which their spirits, like our own, demand and need, they will come back happy and content to be ours "to have and to hold."

3. HELP: Encourage

"To help" our husbands. What do I mean by that? I mean we will use our emerging wholeness to help him become a whole person, too. In a previous chapter I pointed out that *perfect* means *whole*. Our usage of the word *perfect* has distorted the original meaning of the word, so it has become unattainable, and almost negative. But, if we help our husbands to become whole, if we have a concept of them as total persons with souls and spirits as well as bodies, then we will help them be the persons they are capable of being.

As they develop the hidden bits of their beings, we will have the most interesting, exciting, fulfilled husbands in town. We will be envied women! And, what does it cost us? We open up the "cage" in which he may feel confined. But, when he returns to the nest—

our nest—he will be the animated, turned-on creature we first met, courted, married—and more!

There is a lot of truth in the saying, "Marriage is falling in love with a personality, and then living with a character." Or course, *character* can bring to mind a humorously eccentric person, or even one who pretends to be something he is not. But *character* can also refer to the moral and spiritual depth of a person. And those strengths for a husband are developed in marriage, either with or without the help of his spouse. That development depends on the character of his helping—or non-helping spouse!

One woman found herself in a situation where she thought she was in love with another man. She discussed the problem with a very wise friend. Thank goodness she did! She told her friend, who listened with loving support and patience, "I believe I have found a man who will be the perfect husband." This kind listener, with a heart full of compassion and wisdom, answered, "There are no perfect husbands! Caring wives make them!"

May I repeat ever so lovingly and gently, "There are no perfect husbands! Caring wives make them!" Before we can even hope to do that, we ourselves must be whole. We must be in shape!

To get out of shape physically, we don't have to do a thing.
To get out of shape spiritually, we don't have to do a thing.
To get out of shape relationally, we don't have to do a thing.

To become less than a whole person, we don't
have to do a thing.

But, to become a caring wife who wants the best marriage has to offer, we have to do a tremendous
amount! And keep doing, and doing, and doing, and
doing! We can choose to have a marriage that either is
or is not worth the legal paper it is printed on. Either
way, we pay a price. And we are making that choice
right now.

4. HARBOR: Accommodate, protect, give refuge to,
cherish.

Cherish—another one of those dictionary words.
Yet a word which, if put into practice, can "conserve,
protect and restore" our endangered species–husband.

A few years ago I read a book about the "first four
minutes" of encounter between husband and wife,
upon awakening in the morning and again at the time
of each encounter. In those four minutes the quality
of the encounter sets the tone for what follows. One
husband who understood this principle and wanted
to put it into practice expressed his frustration at the
lack of harboring, cherishing, if you will, that he received in return. "More often than not," he said, "I
will put my arms around her only to be pushed away
with a 'Sorry, I'm not in the mood.' I want to make
our marriage like it used to be. I want to respond—not
head toward the bedroom—just respond. But there is
nothing to respond to!" Cherish: "To hold dear, treat
with affection and tenderness."[5] Try it!

5. HEAR: Know

Much literature is written about how to communicate. It seems to have less meaning the more we "hear" about it. "Hear" is in quotes for a reason. We have the notion that to communicate means to talk, that is, to get *our*, *my*, point across. Perhaps the most common complaint a wife levels at her husband is this, "You don't hear a word I'm saying." She is probably right. Her husband turned her off a long time ago.

I have a great-uncle whose wife was a termagant. Once she started her scolding and complaining in the early morning, it went on until he went to bed. When I was little, I couldn't understand why uncle always went to bed so early! As he got older, uncle acquired a hearing problem. He finally acquiesced to the advice of his old cronies and bought a hearing aid. He would pull me up into his lap and tell me stories. He heard everything I said to him. But he did not hear great-aunt. "Why can you hear me and you can't hear auntie, Uncle Frederick?" Uncle chuckled, pulled me close to him and whispered, "When she starts talking I turn my hearing aid off."

The very nature of our society causes each one of us to turn off our hearing aids. Information overkill, noise pollution from super jets and loud music, plus four thousand four hundred and ninety-four minutes of commercials per week on television will turn anybody off. The most often turned-off and tuned-out persons in our noisy world are husband and wife. One communication-starved husband commented: "I don't plan a divorce, but if I did get one, the only way she would know it is if they announced it on 'As the World Turns' !"

Do you ever *listen* to your husband? Do you *hear* him? Do you *know* him? Words may or may not come easy for him, but you, of all the women on earth, are the one woman he has the right to be real with. He may be trying to be real with you. He may be pleading with you. He may be begging you to hear his "insideness." He wants to know you care that he exists, that he has meaning for you, as well as for himself.

Among other things, marriage is a forum where one should be able to express all kinds of thoughts and feelings. Everybody out there in the big wide world is repressing and suppressing because nobody cares about them. In the context of marriage, it is a compliment to be able to turn ourselves inside out to and for our spouse. Where else in the world can we do that?

Most married couples I know agree about many things. Often we are on the same wavelength, but we express and live out our ideologies differently. Our differences are not usually very far apart. How we react, however, is mostly a matter of style. Some husbands and some wives are "hi-fi" persons. They are enthusiastic, excited, hyper-thyroid, decisive and impulsive. They are up and down. That's great! Other husbands and other wives are "low-fi" persons. They take forever to wake up in the morning. They go along smoothly without too many ups and downs. They may be just as enthusiastic, happy or angry about something as their spouse, but their glands respond differently. Or their genes determine for them a more even level of expression. That's great! That is what attracted wife and husband to each other in the first place. They were attracted to those personality traits which complimented their own. It is far more important to think together than to think alike.

Somewhere I read about some research on the speech habits and capacities of men and women. Supposedly, a woman has a word-capability of 34,000 words per day, while a man has a word-capability of 30,000 words per day. How scientific and accurate the "research" is I don't know. But whether we have a greater or lesser word-capability than our man, we can use some of our words to say "I love you" to him, over and over and over and over. Either he will say "I love you, too," or "I don't." But I'll stake this book on the first response and a more exciting relationship because of our effort.

6. HANDLE: Touch

Remember *Tired in Lincoln, Neb.?* She said she had "paid her dues" and "would like to forget about sex all together . . . ." Over 125,000 women wrote back in agreement![6] Personally, I am angry at such distortion of this most intimate kind of love expression. God dignified human sex, and set it apart from animal sex so magnificently—because of all His creatures, humans are the only creatures who face each other in the sex act!

How can we "handle" our husband physically? What about little displays of affection? Holding hands in the automobile while on the way to the grocery store, church, or a trip out of town? What about squeezing his hand while watching television, or caressing his hands and arms with the fingertips? Delicate, light, nonembarrassing nuances that signal a love interlude before a final "good-night." What about some good old-fashioned hugs and kisses before leaving, and upon returning home?

Sometime ago I heard a panel discussing what a man or wife considered the most important room in the house. Immediately I traversed back into time when we lived in an old home in the Midwest. How I planned and thought about making the proper impression for my husband, a professional man. I bought the most expensive wallpaper I could find for the entry, which left bargain basement funds for the rest of the house.

Guests on the panel mentioned the entrance, the hallway, the living room for "impressing," and the dining room for formal entertainment of husband's superiors in corporate organizations. Most of the discussion centered around the room they thought would impress those outside the family!

One panelist, however, had the intestinal fortitude, spelled G-U-T-S to say, "This is incredible! The bedroom in my home is the most important room. It is a retreat for my husband and me. To be together; to read; to watch television; to hold hands quietly; to have our morning coffee (and we take turns in bringing it to each other); to retreat; to make love whenever we feel like it! And we have trained our kids with a "Do Not Disturb" reverence for our sequestered hideaway!" Hooray! This freed the other panelists and one volunteered that she and her husband had agreed to take a morning newspaper instead of the evening edition, because "it's better for sex." Three cheers!

Sexual enjoyment between a husband and wife does not happen naturally. It takes a lifetime of learning and deliberate discovery. Successful instant sex is the invention of fame-oriented pseudo-psychologists. My prescription is to ride in the car on a day that is yours, as husband and wife, together. With no kids or dogs in the back seat! Then talk and talk and talk about everything and anything. Express your feelings of sex, whether they are positive or negative. Suggest to each other ways of making your sexual encounters something special and wonderful, not something to be endured. Then, routinely, when you are home, demonstrate to the kids that affectionately touching your mate and hugging and kissing is a natural thing to do. You are their role models for their life patterns.

There once was a wise man whose fame had spread far and wide. It was said he knew the answer to all questions. A child who had heard of the wise man devised a question designed to stump him. "If I ever get a chance," the child mused, "this is what I'll do. I'll capture a bird and hold it in my hand behind my back. Then I'll ask the wise man, 'What do I have in my hand?' and he will answer, 'You have a bird in your hand.' Then I will ask, 'Is that bird dead or alive?' If he says the bird is dead, I'll hold out my hand, open it and let the bird fly away, showing it's alive. If he says that the bird is alive, I'll quickly squeeze my hand, choke out its life, hold it forth and show it to him dead."

It looked as if the youngster had indeed found a way to successfully challenge the wise man. And, as the story goes, the day came when the child captured a bird and, according to plan, approached the wise man. "What do I have in my hand?" the youngster asked. The wise man replied, "You have a bird in your hand." "Tell me, wise man, is that bird dead or alive?" There was a long pause as the wise man looked at the little one intently. Then he answered, "My child, that depends on you!"

Do we want to take *husband* off the endangered species list? Wives, to a large extent, that depends on us!

Footnotes

Chapter 1   Husbands: In a Race for Survival

1. "How Men Are Changing," *Newsweek,* Jan. 16, 1978, p. 52.
2. "Endangered Species Preservation Act," (PL89-669) 1966. In: United States Statutes at Large, 89th Congress, ed. session, 1966, vol. 80, pt. 1.
3. "India Struggles to Save Her Wildlife," *National Geographic,* vol. 150, no. 3, Sept. 1976, pp. 306–309. (Chart of larger species becoming dangerously low in population.)

Chapter 2   Husbands: The Stronger Sex?

1. *U.S. Statistical Abstracts, 1980,* Bureau of the Census, U.S. Dept. of Commerce, no. 106, p. 72.
2. Ibid.
3. *Los Angeles Times,* Feb. 10, 1974, Part I, p. 4.
4. *U.S. Abstracts,* no. 106, p. 72.
5. Herb Goldberg, *The Hazards of Being Male,* (New York: Nash Publishing, 1976), p. 180.
6. Lois Wladis Hoffman, "Changes in Family Roles, Socialization and Sex Differences," *American Psychologist,* Aug. 1977, p. 648.
7. Ibid.
8. Ibid., p. 647.
9. Todd Tieger, "On the Biological Basis of Sex Differences in Aggression," *Child Development,* vol. 51, no. 4, p. 957.
10. Bonnie R. Seegmiller, "Sex-Typed Behavior in Preschoolers: Sex, Age, and Social Class Effects," *The Journal of Psychology,* 1980, no. 104, pp. 31–33; Arnold D. LeUnes, Jack R. Nation and Nikila M. Turley, "Male-Female Performance in Learned

Helplessness," *The Journal of Psychology*, 1980, no. 104, pp. 255–258.

11. Goldberg, *The Hazards of Being Male*, p. 183.
12. Ibid., p. 188.
13. Prayer of *Alcoholics Anonymous*.

Chapter 3   Husbands: Their Territory Threatened

1. "How Men Are Changing," Newsweek, Jan. 16, 1978, p. 52.
2. David M. Schneider and Kathleen Gaough, eds., *Matrilineal Kinship*, (Berkeley and Los Angeles: University of California Press, 1961), pp. 1–29, of the Introduction.
3. Deuteronomy 21:5, 21:15–17, 24:1–4. Numbers Chapter 26 describes in painstaking detail the patrilineal descent. The entire Old Testament is "patrilineai," in the sense that from Abraham on to Jesus, the line is through the male, and "patriarchal" i.e., through the father, in custom.
4. Katherine of Aragon of Spain, Henry VIII's first wife, married him to strengthen ties between Spain and England. Marie Antoinette was married to Louis XVI to steady a shaky alliance between Austria and France. History is replete with such alliances.
5. Sheila M. Rothman, *Woman's Proper Place*, (New York: Basic Books, 1978), from the Introduction pp. 1–9.
6. Ibid., p. 23.
7. Ibid.
8. Ibid., (Quote from Ehrenreich and English, *Complaints and Disorders*, New York, 1973), p. 19.
9. Rothman, *Proper Place*, p. 26.
10. Ibid., from the Introduction, pp. 1–9.
11. Betty Friedan, *The Feminine Mystique*, (New York: Dell Publishing Co., 1963), p. 53.
12. Roberta Hestenes, "Culture, Counterculture and Christian Transformation," *Theology, News and Notes*, Published for Fuller Theological Seminary, vol. XXI, no. 2, p. 20.
13. *U.S. Statistical Abstracts, 1980*, Bureau of the Census, U.S. Dept. of Commerce, no. 106, p. 18, (40.2% of the population over 3 yrs. moved between 1975 and 1979.)
14. Betty Friedan, *The Second Stage*, (New York: Simon and Schuster, 1981), pp. 125, 126.

Chapter 4   Husbands: Chauvinist or Chauvinized?

1. Proverbs 31:10–12, 28b, 29.
2. *Webster's 3rd New International Dictionary,* (Springfield, Massachusetts: G. and C. Merriam Co., 1976).
3. David M. Schneider and Kathleen Gaough, eds., *Matrilineal Kinship,* (Berkeley and Los Angeles: University of California Press, 1961), from the Introduction, pp. 1–29.
4. Arnold D. LeUnes, Jack R. Nation and Nikila M. Turley, "Male-Female Performance in Learned Helplessness," *The Journal of Psychology,* 1980, no. 104, p. 258.
5. LaVerne R. Graf, Program Specialist, Special Education, Sacramento City Schools
6. Todd Tieger, "On the Biological Basics of Sex Differences in Aggression," *Child Development,* vol. 51, no. 4, Dec. 1980, p. 958.
7. Natalie Gittelson, *Dominus: A Woman Looks at Men's Lives,* (New York: Farrar, Straus and Giroux, 1978), pp. 20, 21.
8. Genesis 2:7, 18, 24.

Chapter 5   Husbands: It's O.K. to Cry!

1. Marc Feigen Fasteau, "The Male Machine: The High Price of Macho," *Psychology Today,* Sept. 1975, p. 60.
2. James Wagenvoord, ed., *Men: A Book for Women,* (New York: Avon Books, 1980), p. 42, 44.
3. Fasteau, "The Male Machine," p. 60a.
4. "Death Stuns Police Force," *Bakersfield Californian,* June 21, 1980, Section I, p. 1.
5. Wagenvoord, *Men,* p. 36.
6. Excerpt from "Have You Touched Anyone Lately?," by Sidney B. Simon, Reader's Digest Condensation, May 1980, from *Caring, Feeling, Touching,* (Allen, Texas: Argus Communications, 1976). "For information about current Values Realization materials and a schedule of nationwide training workshops, contact Sidney B. Simon, Old Mountain Rd. Hadley, MA 01035." (Publisher's note: This does not imply endorsement by the author or the publisher.)
7. Wagenvoord, *Men,* p. 165.
8. John 11:35
9. Psalm 6:6
10. Psalm 69:3

11. Psalm 70:2, 3
12. Psalm 71:9

**Chapter 6   Husbands:Their Cycles, Moods and
                Rhythms**

1. *The American Heritage Dictionary of the English Language*, Wm. Moore, ed., (Boston: Houghton Mifflin Co., 1978).
2. *Our Magnificent Wildlife: How to enjoy and preserve it*, Reader's Digest, 1975, pp. 344–368.
3. Ann Guilfoyle with Edward R. Ricciuti, *Peaceable Kingdom*, (Reader's Digest, June 1980), published by Macmillan Publishing Co., Inc., Copyright by AG Editions, 1979.
4. Mary Brown Parlee, "The Rhythm in Men's Lives," *Psychology Today*, April 1978, p. 82–91.
5. Rosetta Reitz, *Menopause: A Positive Approach*, (Radnor, Pennsylvania: Chilton Book Co., 1977), p. 228.
6. Parlee, "The Rhythm in Men's Lives," p. 82.
7. Michael H. Chase, "Every 90 Minutes a Brainstorm," *Psychology Today*, November 1979, p. 172.
8. Richard Grossman, "I Got Rhythm and So Do You," *Family Health Magazine*, March, 1979, p. 54.
9. Dr. Donald R. Forden, Family and Marriage Counselor, Bakersfield Counseling Group.
10. Edward Ziegler, "Does the Moon Control Your Moods?" Reader's Digest, March 1980. Based on *The Lunar Effect* by Arnold L. Lieber, M.D., produced by Jerome B. Agel Anchor Press/Doubleday & Co., Inc.; *Moodswing* by Ronald R. Fieve, M.D. William Morrow & Co., Inc.; and *Lifetide*, by Lyall Watson, Simon and Schuster, Inc.
11. Ibid., p. 96.
12. Ibid., p. 97.
13. Rex Hersey, "Feele und Gefichel des Arbeiters, psychologie der Menschen Fuhrung," von Prof. Dr. Rexford B. Hersey, (mit einen geleitwort von reichsorgen isationsleiter, Dr. Robert Ley), (Leipzig: Konkordia/Verlag, 1935).
14. Parlee, "The Rhythm in Men's Lives," p. 82.
15. Ibid., p. 85.
16. Ibid., p. 86.
17. Ecclesiastes 3:1–8.

Chapter 7   Husbands: Within a Dark Wood

1. Dr. Daniel J. Levinson, *The Seasons of a Man's Life*, (New York: Alfred A. Knopf, 1978), p. 239.
2. Ibid., p. 7.
3. Ibid., pp. 209, 210.
4. Helmut J. Ruebsaat, M.D. and Raymond Hull, *The Male Climacteric*, (New York: E. P. Dutton, 1975), from the jacket.
5. Jim Conway, *Men in Mid-life Crisis*, (Elgin, Illinois: David C. Cook Publishing Co., 1978), pp. 11, 12.
6. "The Mid-Life: In a Dark Wood," *Christian Medical Society Journal*, vol. X, no. 3, p. 3.
7. Robert H. Williams, M.D., ed. *Textbook of Endocrinology*, 5th ed., p. 346 Article on "The Testes," 5th paragraph. (W. B. Saunders Co.: Philadelphia, 1974).
8. Genesis 1:27b.
9. John P. Hayes, Associated Press, "American Male Image Changing," *Bakersfield Californian*, June 17, 1979.
10. Theodore Rubin, M.D., *Understanding Your Mate*, (New York: Ballantine Books, 1978), p. 123.
11. Levinson, *The Seasons of a Man's Life*, p. 210.
12. Dr. W. A. Nolen, M.D., "What You Should Know About Male Menopause!," *McCall's*, June 1980, pp. 84–88.
13. Ruebsaat and Hull, *The Male Climacteric*, pp. 8–28.
14. Nolen, "What You Should Know About Male Menopause!," p. 153.
15. "The Mid-Life: In a Dark Wood," p. 8.
16. Levinson, *The Seasons of a Man's Life*, p. 215.
17. II Samuel, Chapters 10 and 11.
18. II Samuel 11:1.
19. "Growing Older," *Health Facts*, vol. VII, no. 34, March 1982, pp. 4, 5.
20. Hayes, "American Male Image Changing," p. A4.
21. Anne Morrow Lindbergh, *Gift From the Sea*, (New York: Vintage Books, 1955), pp. 84, 85.

Chapter 8   Husbands: They Also Have Other Choices

1. Natalie Gittelson, *Dominus, A Woman Looks at Men's Lives*, (New York: Farrar, Straus and Giroux, 1978), pp. 20, 21.
2. *U.S. Statistical Abstract*, 1980, 101st ed., U.S. Department of Commerce, Bureau of the Census, no. 54, p. 43.

3. Dr. Daniel J. Levinson, *The Seasons of a Man's Life*, (New York: Alfred A. Knopf, 1978), pp. 72–77, 106, 107.
4. Richard Schickel, "The Great Second Chance," *Esquire*, March 1980, vol. 93, no. 3, p. 47.
5. "Herpes: The New Sexual Leprosy," *Time*, July 28, 1980, p. 76.

Chapter 9   Husbands: Sex—Strife and Serenity

1. Jim Sanderson, "Refiguring a Sexual Equation," *Los Angeles Times*, part VII, October 19, 1980, p. 22. Reprinted through permission of Sun Features, Inc.
2. Ibid.
3. Violet Franks and Bosonti Burtle, eds., *Women in Therapy: New Psychotherapies*, (New York: Brunner-Nozel, 1974), p. 5.
4. *Encyclopaedia Britannica*, vol. 19, s.v. "Victoria."
5. Catherine Marshall, *Something More*, (Lincoln, VA: Chosen Books, 1974), pp. 73–76.
6. Jim Sanderson, "Refiguring a Sexual Equation," p. 22.
7. John Allan Lavender, *Marriage at Its Best*, (Denver: Accent Books, 1982), p. 85.
8. Masters and Johnson, *The Pleasure Bond*, (Boston: Little, Brown & Co., 1974), p. 85.
9. "A Potent Myth," *Time*, February 25, 1980, p. 59.
10. Richard F. Sparks, M.D., Robert A. White, Peter B. Connolly, M.S., "Impotence Is Not Always Psychogenic," *Journal of American Medical Association*, February 22/29, 1980, vol. 243, no. 8, p. 750.

Chapter 10   Husbands: Whole Is Better Than Perfect

1. Genesis 2:24.
2. "Growth Must Not Stop in Marriage," from a lecture by Dr. Roger Gould, psychiatrist, UCLA.
3. "Be ye perfect." Matthew 5:48. In the Greek the word is "telos" (perfect), and refers to one's end goal toward which one strives. Jesus said in essence "Make it the goal of your life to grow up in every area and become whole in every sense of the word."
4. Hannah Whitall Smith, *The Christian's Secret of a Happy Life*, (Old Tappan, New Jersey: Fleming H. Revell, 1974).
5. Matthew 6:28.

6. Matthew 6:29.
7. Psalms 18:19.
8. Romans 8:35–39.
9. See John 5:1–8.
10. John 10:10.
11. John 3:6.
12. Ibid.
13. John 3:7.
14. Based on Dr. John Allan Lavender's teaching cassette album, "Spiritual Gifts," available through Project Winsome Publishers, P.O. Box 111, Bakersfield, California 93302

Chapter 11   Husbands: How to Preserve the Species
1. Anne Morrow Lindbergh, *Gift from the Sea*, (New York: Vintage Books, Edition 1965), p. 108.
2. This epoch is recorded in its entirety in Joshua 3:1–4:18.
3. Alfred Tennyson, 1809–1892, from "Ulysses."
4. Matthew 16:25, Matthew 25:40 (Author's paraphrase).
5. *American Heritage Dictionary*, Wm. Morris, ed., (Boston: Houghton Mifflin Co., 1978).
6. Jim Sanderson, "Refiguring a Sexual Equation," *Los Angeles Times*, part VIII, October 19, 1980, p. 22. Reprinted through permission of Sun Features, Inc.